TOKYO

Pierre Mustière and Yoko Kera

JONGLEZ PUBLISHING

travel guides

Pierre Mustière was born in France in 1976, but has lived in Tokyo since 1998. He has a keen interest in the city's history and is always curious to learn more about it. At weekends he often wanders around little-known corners of the Japanese capital in search of a forgotten bridge, an obscure alley, or a hidden shrine or garden, to discover (or rediscover) parts of this metropolis that he thought he knew. Although working in a completely different field in his day job, for his own pleasure he has qualified as a National Guide-Interpreter (通訳案内士) and is also licensed as a Tokyo City Guide (東京シティガイド).

Yoko Kera (良 曜 子 子) comes from the island of Sado in the Sea of Japan. She moved to the capital to study at the prestigious University of Tokyo (Todai), and is more interested in the city's hipper sites and the latest international influences than in its past.

Pierre and Yoko are married and have one daughter.

We have taken great pleasure in drawing up *Secret Tokyo* and hope that through its guidance you will, like us, continue to discover unusual, hidden or little-known aspects of the city.

Descriptions of certain places are accompanied by thematic sections highlighting historical details or anecdotes as an aid to understanding the city in all its complexity.

Secret Tokyo also draws attention to the multitude of details found in places that we may pass every day without noticing. These are an invitation to look more closely at the urban landscape and, more generally, a means of seeing our own city with the curiosity and attention that we often display while travelling elsewhere …

Comments on this guidebook and its contents, as well as information on places we may not have mentioned, are more than welcome and will enrich future editions.

Don't hesitate to contact us:
E-mail: info@jonglezpublishing.com
Jonglez Publishing
25 rue du Maréchal Foch
78000 Versailles, France

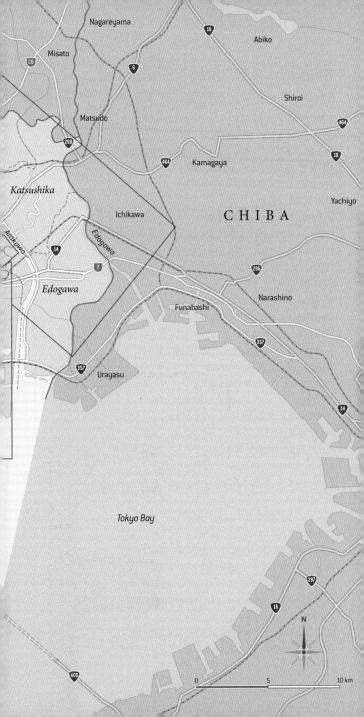

CONTENTS

Minato / Chiyoda / Chuo

Ota / Shinagawa / Meguro

Setagaya / Suginami / Nakano

CONTENTS

Nerima / Itabashi / Kita

CONTENTS

Shibuya / Shinjuku

Edogawa / Katsushika / Adachi

Bunkyo / Toshima

CONTENTS

Arakawa / Taito / Sumida

Koto

Minato / Chiyoda / Chuo

CRIMINOLOGY SECTION OF MEIJI UNIVERSITY MUSEUM

Torture of all kinds

1-1 Kanda-Surugadai, Chiyoda-ku (東京都千代田区神田駿河台 1-1)
5-minute walk from Ochanomizu (御茶ノ水) or Shin-Ochanomizu (新御茶ノ水) stations, JR Sobu or Chuo lines; Tokyo metro Marunouchi or Chiyoda lines
Open 10am–5pm, closed Sundays, public holidays, during school summer holidays (August 10-16) and December 26 to January 7
Admission free

The museum of the private Meiji University, in the basement of the Academy Common building on Surugadai campus, is divided into three main sections. Although the archaeological and consumer goods sections are interesting, the most surprising area, located between the other two, is devoted to criminology (刑事博物館) and has an extensive collection of objects relating to the history of legislation, legal judgments and sentences. Notable among the attractions are detailed illustrations of the torture practices in the Edo period along with the "tools" used. Execution methods – more or less ingenious depending on the severity of the crime – are also shown by sometimes very graphic illustrations, including spectacular old photographs. The severity of penalties at the time may seem extreme

today. The museum has the only example of a Virgin of Nuremberg (Maiden)[1] in Japan, as well as a guillotine, although they are early 20th century replicas. Old legal manuscripts, edicts written on wooden boards and instruments used to capture fugitives in the Edo era complete this unusual collection. Various other torture devices are exhibited in this museum with its rather special atmosphere – not recommended for sensitive souls, as a notice warns. It fully deserves its nickname, "museum of torture".

[1] *Instrument of torture in the form of a coffin with the face of a maiden, the inside of which is covered with long metal spikes.*

PILLARS INDICATING
THE SAKUMA BRIDGE SITE

②

A bridge with no water on the way out of Akihabara

1 Kanda-Sakumachi, Chiyoda-ku (東京都千代田区神田佐久間町 1)
5 minutes from Akihabara station (秋葉原), Tokyo metro Hibiya line;
JR Yamanote, Sobu or Keihin Tohoku lines; MIR Tsukuba express
Accessible 24/7

At the south exit of Akihabara station, between Yodobashi and the Kandagawa, pillars indicating the site of the bridge stand on the south side of Akihabara Park and on the other side of the avenue towards the river. These pillars, all engraved with the name of the bridge they represent, are a reminder of Sakumabashi (佐久間橋 – Sakuma Bridge). Curiously enough, there doesn't seem to be any water to cross.

There's a historical explanation for this. At first, Akihabara was a multimodal transport hub: cargo was transported by boat on the Kandagawa, then brought to the station along a narrow canal dug in the late 19th century (blocked up in the 1960s) and crossed by the vanished bridge. Towards the end of the Meiji era, Akihabara was the city's second busiest freight station. It was only opened to passengers in 1925.

Well before being a benchmark for electronics, the district was mainly used by timber merchants. One of them was Sakuma Heihachi,[1] who gave his name to the bridge and the neighbourhood.

Tiny Akihabara

The neon lights around Akihabara station are not in the district of that name but are scattered in several Chiyoda districts (Kanda-Sakumacho, Kanda-Hirakawacho, Kanda-Matsunagacho, Kanda-Hanaokacho, Kanda-Aioicho, Kanda-Neribeicho and Soto-Kanda). The administrative district of Akihabara, in Taito ward, is on the fringes of the electronic hurly-burly, about 500 metres north of the station. It's just a row of fairly nondescript blocks along the railway line, far from what you might imagine.

[1] 佐久間平八, ?–?, *flourished early 17th century.*

TRAIN OBSERVATION PLATFORM MAACH ECUTE KANDA MANSEIBASHI

Observatory on the renovated platforms of a former station

1-25-4 Kanda-Sudacho, Chiyoda-ku (東京都千代田区神田須田町 1-25-4)
5-minute walk from Akihabara station (秋葉原), Tokyo metro Hibiya line,
JR Yamanote, Sobu or Keihin Tohoku lines; MIR Tsukuba express
Open (observation platform): 11am–10.30pm Monday to Saturday,
11am–8.30pm Sundays and public holidays

Right next to Akihabara, the former Manseibashi station (closed in 1943) was renovated and reopened in September 2013 as a commercial complex, mAAch Ecute Kanda Manseibashi (マーチエキュート神田万世橋). The development reuses some structural elements of the station, including its red bricks.

MAAch Ecute houses a few restaurants, shops and some rather nice cafés, but the major interest of a visit is a trip across the station platforms, converted into a viewing platform to watch the trains travelling on the Chuo line. The platform is glazed, so you can enjoy the spectacle quietly. A café has been installed in part of the renovated platforms for anyone who wants a snack while watching the goods trains. Access is by two original flights of steps, one dating from 1935 and other 1912. The fairly late closing times and well-thought-out lighting let you enjoy the night trains with the lights of Akihabara gleaming in the background. With the frequent traffic on the Chuo line, this is a guaranteed spectacle.

Manseibashi station, opened in 1912, was the first Chuo terminus. Designed by Tatsuno Kingo,[1] Manseibashi lost its importance after the 1919 opening of Tokyo station, also by Kingo. The original station building, which burned down during the 1923 earthquake, was reconstructed but not in its original style. After the opening of Kanda and Akihabara stations, attendance dropped and the station was closed down in 1943. It was replaced by a railway museum, which in its turn closed in 2006.

Manseibashi ghost station

Underground, between Kanda and Suehirocho on the Ginza line, there is also a Manseibashi subway station that was only open for two years, between 1930 and 1931. This station is closed to the public, but an extremely close look from the windows of the Ginza subway will reveal a variation in the frequency of the tunnel support pillars on the way to Kanda. The ventilation shafts are still there, under the grilles on Chuo-dori sidewalk, near the Laox store in Akihabara.

[1] 辰野金吾, *1854–1919. Meiji architect.*

STATUETTE OF DAIKOKUTEN AT MINOBU-BETSUIN

Oily statue

Minobu-Betsuin temple
3-2 Nihonbashi-Kodenmacho, Chuo-ku (東京都中央区日本橋小伝馬町 3-2)
2 minutes from Kondenmacho station (小伝馬町), Tokyo metro Hibiya line

Inside the small temple of Minobu-Betsuin (身延別院), not to be confused with its larger neighbour Daianrakuji, you'll notice a plump and shiny statuette of *Daikokuten*.

This is one of the few Aburakake-Daikokuten (油掛大黒天 – Daikoku to be Sprinkled with Oil) in the country and the only one in Tokyo.

Traditionally oil has to be poured over the statue for good auspices, so its shiny appearance is no surprise. This statue isn't very old. Just after

the war, the wife of actor Hasegawa Kazuo,[1] who was particularly devout, saw Daikokuten in a dream and spoke about it at the temple.

The temple then erected this statue, so Tokyoites could also venerate him as he deserved. The statue is surrounded by oil – just use the ladle supplied to pour some over it.

The temple also has a commemorative stone erected in 1983 by a local group of restaurants selling *kabayaki*, a local speciality, to give thanks for the fish from which the restauranteurs make their living.

[1] 長谷川一夫, *1908–1984. Theatre and cinema actor (appeared in some 300 films), particularly in the 1940s and 50s.*

NEARBY
Kokucho bell

⑤

Just opposite Minobu-Betsuin, Jisshi-koen is laid out on the site of Denmacho prison from the Edo period. In the middle of the park, a small concrete tower houses the Kokucho bell (石町時の鐘). This bell, originally sited about 200 metres away, has been repeatedly destroyed by fire and the current model dates from 1711. Its chimes were also used to signal the time for prison executions. Nowadays the bell is only rung on the first day of the year. This is one of the nine bells of Edo installed to indicate the time of day for residents – it was the city's first. There are still two other antique bells, one in Ueno Park (near the face of the Buddha, see p. 246) and one in the temple of Senso-ji at Asakusa. The six others (Honjo, Yokoyamamachi, Ichigaya-Yawata, Meguro-Fudo, Akasaka-Tamachi and Yotsuya) have been lost.

Doing time in Edo

The traditional way of sounding the hour in the Edo period differed significantly from modern practices.

The day was divided into twelve "hours" associated with the Chinese signs of the zodiac (six nocturnal, six diurnal) of varying length, depending on the amount of daylight and therefore the seasons.

The hours were counted from 9, the ninth hour corresponding to midnight and midday, down to 4, the last hour of the morning and last hour before midnight (in other words, in order from midnight, 9, 8, 7, 6, 5, 4, 9, 8, 7, 6, 5, 4).

The sixth hours marked the imminent sunrise and sunset. The bells initially rang three times, then sounded the hour, changing pace.

The Meiji Government finally adopted Western practices in 1872, with consistent times for 24 hours each day, paving the way for some difficult transition months for the citizens.

Automatically sounding hours of varying lengths was a major engineering challenge.

It gave rise to some impressive mechanical devices, such as Tanaka Hisashige's[1] universal clock dating from 1851, displayed at the National Museum of Nature and Science in Ueno Park.

---

[1] 田中久重, 1799–1881. Engineer and founder in 1875 of Shibaura Seisakusho (芝浦製作所), which became Toshiba in 1939 in a merger with Tokyo Denki. A reproduction of the universal clock is on display at Toshiba Science Museum in Kawasaki.

PASONA GROUP URBAN FARM

Farm offices

2-6-4 Otemachi, Chiyoda-ku (東京都千代田区大手町 2-6-4)
Otemachi station (大手町), Tokyo metro Hanzomon, Tozai, Marunouchi
or Chiyoda lines; Toei subway Mita line
Open 10.30am–5pm, closed weekends and public holidays
The farm is to move sometimes soon, check http://www.pasona-nouentai.co.jp/

Pasona O2 Urban Farm, by the Pasona employment agency, occupied the former underground vaults of the Daiwa Bank, which ceased trading in 2003. In 2010, Pasona O2 closed down, the group's offices moved to the present site and their know-how was extended to the entire building, pushing the concept of coexistence between nature and office work, to create the aptly named Pasona Group Urban Farm (パソナグループアーバンファーム).

The renovated 1950s building, whose façade is covered in greenery and flowering plants, is easily spotted from the street. The 200 species of plants on the exterior walls serve as natural insulation, retaining heat in winter and keeping the interior cool in summer. Two floors of the building are partially open to the public and can be visited without advance booking.

On the ground floor, an artificial swamp of 90 square metres (which is again in use as a rice field after a temporary closure following the 2011 earthquake) is lit by halogen and sodium lamps. A flower meadow inside adds a little colour in all seasons, while a variety of plants are cultivated on shelves artificially lit by a mixture of fluorescent lamps. Sometimes you can see cucumbers and gourds hanging from the ceiling. Even the second-floor toilets have a touch of the jungle.

Around eighty species of plants are grown on the premises by the employees. Vegetables from the urban farm are used to supply the canteen. The upper floors and roof are not accessible to the public, but are also used to make this whole building an unusual example of an office-farm in the city centre.

COMMEMORATIVE STONE AT WILLIAM ADAMS' RESIDENCE

The shogun's English advisor for foreign affairs

11-10 Nihonbashi-Muromachi, Chuo-ku (東京都中央区日本橋室町 1-10)
5-minute walk from Mitsukoshi-mae station (三越前), Tokyo metro Ginza
or Hanzomon lines
Accessible 24/7

The site of the Edo house of the English navigator William Adams (三浦按針屋敷跡), in Japanese Miura Anjin (三浦按針 – the Navigator of Miura), is marked by a sober grey stone not far from the Mitsukoshi department store and the Bank of Japan.

The stone is set back from the sidewalk, wedged next to a jeweller's premises, so it's easy to miss. The street still bears his name, Anjin-dori (按針通り).

A commemorative stone was first erected in 1930, but it was destroyed during the war. This one dates from 1951.

Miura Anjin, the first Western samurai

The fascinating life of William Adams was fictionalized by James Clavell in his book *Shogun*, adapted for television in the eponymous series, where he was played (under another name) by Richard Chamberlain. Arriving in Japan in 1600, a few months before the battle of Sekigahara, as a pilot on a drifting Dutch ship, Adams won the confidence of Tokugawa Ieyasu. Ieyasu became the first Tokugawa shogun in 1603 with Adams as his advisor on foreign affairs. Adams was appointed a *hatamoto*, took the name of Miura Anjin and became the first Western samurai. On the death of Ieyasu in 1616, Adams lost his influence with the shogunate and was confined to Hirado, at Nagasaki, as the country gradually entered its period of isolation from the rest of the world. He died in 1620.

NEARBY
Nihonbashi Uogashi memorial
Before Tsukiji (8)

Not far from the stone marking the Adams residence, along Kandagawa towards No. 1-10 and next to a subway entrance, is a little statue of a seated woman. This discreet monument, erected in 1953, marks the site of Nihonbashi Uogashi (日本橋魚河岸), the ancient fish market of Edo and Tokyo. This market, badly damaged during the 1923 earthquake, had to move to Tsukiji, laying the foundations of the modern fish market. There's not much left now of what used to be one of the animated centres of Edo's economy.

MEMORIAL TO THE HEAD OF TAIRA NO MASAKADO

The message is clear: don't disturb Masakado

1-2-1 Otemachi, Chiyoda-ku (東京都千代田区大手町 1-2-1)
5-minute walk from Otemachi station (大手町), Tokyo metro Hanzomon,
Marunouchi, Tozai or Chiyoda lines; Toei subway Mita line
Accessible 24/7

At the heart of the business district where the major financial and commercial companies are housed, a slender memorial stands in a shady spot known as the mound of the head of Taira no Masakado (平将門の首塚). It's dedicated to the head of the man who became the city's guardian deity (*shugoshin*), worshipped among other places at Kanda-Myojin shrine.

According to one of the Masakado legends, the warrior's head is said

to have flown by itself from Kyoto (Heian-Kyo at the time) to Kanto in search of his body. It landed here on what was probably a mound near Kofun, then on the edge of the bay, before Tokyo was extended.

The site is highly respected and carefully maintained to avoid angering the deity, with recent offerings lined up at the foot of the commemorative stone. Anecdotes, unfortunate coincidences, superstitions, rumours of curses and other legends abound about those who've risked the wrath of Masakado.

After the 1923 earthquake, the tumulus (then much higher) was replaced by temporary buildings of the Ministry of Finance, which had burned down after the quake. The minister died and so, it seems, did several people directly involved in the work. The buildings ended up on fire, struck by lightning during a violent storm. After the war, the memorial site was supposed to have been replaced by a parking space for the Allied headquarters, but the death of a bulldozer operator interrupted the work. The message is clear: don't disturb Masakado.

Inside the memorial are numerous statues of frogs (蛙 – *kaeru*), placed there as offerings to request the safe return (帰る – *kaeru*, to return) of an employee transferred abroad or a missing friend, taking a lead from the return of Masakado's head to Kanto.

Taira no Masakado

Taira no Masakado (平将門), a noble from the Kanto region, was the instigator of one of the largest armed revolts against central government in the mid-10th century.

Following a succession of conflicts with other local nobles, apparently with no direct link with the Kyoto court, in 940 Masakado took direct control of much of the region, and in passing overthrew the governor of Hitachi province. Kyoto then demanded an end to what was becoming a threat to the central government and an army led by Taira no Sadamori[1] and Fujiwara no Hidesato,[2] greatly outnumbering the Kanto rebels, crushed the revolt. Masakado was beheaded and his head brought to Kyoto to be displayed for two nights and three days.

Over the centuries the name of Masakado became a legend, and many superstitions and folktales reflecting the opposition between Kanto and Kansai grew up around him. He was deified at Kanda-Myojin in 1309, and the shrine became the protector of Edo during the Tokugawa shogunate.

---

[1] 平貞盛, ?–989, Taira no Masakado's cousin, whose father (Masakado's uncle) was killed in 935 during a battle involving Masakado.
[2] 藤原秀郷, ?–?, nobleman and general, see also p. 274.

CHINREISHA

The other shrine to war dead

3-1-1 Kudan-Kita, Chiyoda-ku (東京都千代田区九段北 3-1-1)
10-minute walk from Kudanshita station (九段下), Tokyo metro Hanzomon
or Tozai lines; Toei subway Shinjuku line
Yasukuni shrine grounds open at 6am; close at 5pm January and December,
6pm March, April, September and October, 7pm May to August
Chinreisha: you can approach the shrine with a priest's permission (ask a miko,
or "shrine maiden") provided you are accompanied; this is officially for security
reasons

Behind the Yasukuni Shinto shrine is another small shrine or *hokora*, Chinreisha (鎮霊社 – Spirit Pacifying Shrine), erected in 1965 on the initiative of the head priest, Prince Tsukuba Fujimaro.[1]

The main Yasukuni shrine is dedicated to all those who died in the service of the emperor after the Meiji era, including some very controversial figures. The small and often overlooked Chinreisha honours the *kami* (spirits) of all victims of the horrors of war, regardless of nationality. It thus offers sanctuary to the dead who would not have found a place in the main shrine, such as atomic bomb or US bombing victims, or even Saigo Takamori.[2]

Like the main shrine, Chinreisha carries (very) heavy political overtones and sometimes causes controversy and extremist actions.

Late on 31 December 2014, an apparently suicidal young man tried to burn down the shrine, which was seriously damaged but has since been restored. Remember: to visit Chinreisha to pay your respects, first ask a priest.

NEARBY

Pillars of Yasukuni main gate ⑪

Traces of arson

Yasukuni shrine, where the *kami* of the 2.4 million who died for the emperor are revered, crystallizes nationalist passions between Japan and some of its Asian neighbours.

The toilets on the south side were the scene of a minor bomb attack in November 2015 in which fortunately nobody was injured. The main gate of the shrine, decorated with the imperial seal, still bears the traces of an arson attempt by a Chinese activist in late December 2011 on a pillar to the left (facing the shrine).

Statues of animals killed in wartime ⑫

The northern part of the shrine enclosure, next to the white Yushukan building devoted to military history, contains three animal statues: a dog, a horse and a carrier pigeon.

These statues were erected to appease the spirits of animals killed in wartime. The horse in the centre dates from 1958. The plaque beneath the statue says that about 1 million horses perished in wars from the Meiji era to the end of the Pacific War. The pigeon has been there since 1982 and the German shepherd dog since 1992.

Facing the shrine, right next to the animal statues, a Noh theatre stage from the Meiji era was installed in the grounds of the shrine in 1903. Performances are regularly given to distract the spirits. This stage is thought to be the oldest in the city.

---

[1] 筑波藤麿, *1905–1978, fifth head priest of the shrine from 1946.*
[2] 西 郷 隆盛, *1828–1877, samurai during the Meiji Restoration, died in the Satsuma rebellion. Saigo is the main inspiration for the Katsumoto character in the film,* The Last Samurai *(see Police Museum, p. 31).*

TAKARAKUJI DREAMKAN

How much do 100 million yen weigh?

2-5-7 Kyobashi, Chuo-ku (東京都中央区京橋 2-5-7)
2-minute walk from Kyobashi station (京橋), Tokyo metro Ginza line;
or 2 minutes from Takaracho station (宝町), Toei subway Asakusa line
Open 10am–7.30pm Monday, Tuesday, Thursday and Friday, 10am–7pm
Wednesday, 10am–6pm Saturday; closed Sundays and public holidays –
if a public holiday falls on a Sunday, closed the following day; closed
29 December to 3 January; if the draw takes place on a public holiday,
the centre opens at 5pm
Draws open to the public at 6.45pm – audience capacity thirty
Admission free

Dedicated to the national lottery, Tokyo's Takarakuji Dreamkan (宝くじドリーム館) reopened in 2004 after a major renovation. In a large, brightly lit room, under the watchful eye of Ku-chan, the lottery mascot, are a few exhibits more or less connected to the game. Darts, lotto tickets with various designs, lotteries around the world, fill the display cases near the entrance.

There is also the famous brochure distributed to the winners of prizes in excess of 10 million yen: *Sono hi kara yomu hon* (「その日」から読む本 – The Book to Read after D-Day). You can also try to lift the equivalent weight of 100 million yen in 10,000 yen notes, and realize that 400 million, even in 10,000 yen notes, take up a lot of space. In other words, the "dream" is at hand, almost…

The centre, which is open to the public free of charge, is also used for lottery draws that are held behind a large screen made of reinforced glass. These draws are usually held at 6.45pm and you can attend, although there's only room for thirty people.

NEARBY

Tokyo Metropolitan Police Museum ⑭
Chez Pipo-kun

Well guarded by Pipo-kun, the noble mascot of the metropolitan police at 3-5-1 Kyobashi, the Police Museum (警察博物館) offers 3- to 12-year-olds, both girls and boys, a friendly opportunity to wear police uniform, on request.

First though, the children (or their parents) will have to answer some basic questions: do they want a standard or a motorbike uniform? And what colour: red or blue? Obviously helmets are provided and you can take a souvenir photo on a real motorbike. Aspiring pilots can sit in the cockpit of a police helicopter from the 1950s.

Exhibitions on the second and third floors, which treat the history of the country's police force more seriously, will probably be of more interest to adults. They are much less popular than the ground floor, with the vehicles (motorbikes, etc.) that are so popular with children. There are, for example, historical uniforms, swords, a brief presentation of heroes killed in the course of duty and an explanation of the role of the imperial police during the Satsuma rebellion. A shield used during the Asama chalet[1] incident, with some impressive bullet holes, is on display.

The fourth floor, rather busier than the second and third, presents modern police signs and standard equipment. You can test a driving simulator, provided you have a valid Japanese driving licence.

Kawaji Toshiyoshi, Saigo Takamori and the Satsuma rebellion

The Satsuma rebellion (which freely inspired the film *The Last Samurai*), led by Saigo Takamori, was the last major armed revolt of disaffected samurai against the new imperial government, nine years after the Meiji Restoration. Kawaji Toshiyoshi, who like Saigo came from Satsuma, was the founder of modern policing. He came to Tokyo after the restoration on the recommendation of Saigo himself. Having travelled in Europe, in 1874 he founded a police system inspired by what he'd observed in France. At the time of the rebellion in 1877, Kawaji was involved in the fight against the mutineers of his homeland, convinced of the need to maintain order. He fell ill and died in 1879. His uniform and sword are on display in the museum.

---

[1] 浅間山荘事件, *taken hostage from 19 to 28 February 1972 by a far-left group in a cottage near Karuizawa (three dead), which strongly influenced the history of television and journalism in Japan. The events of 28 February, broadcast live, attracted record audiences.*

OKUNO BUILDING AT GINZA
A touch of old Paris

1-9-8 Ginza, Chuo-ku (東京都中央区銀座 1-9-8)
5 minutes from Ginza-itchome station (銀座一丁目), Tokyo metro Yurakucho line
Opening hours vary according to gallery

The Okuno building (奥野ビル), completed in 1932 in the back streets of Ginza, is one of the rare remaining examples of a luxury apartment block from the early Showa era. Having kept all its splendour, it happily brings to life the Ginza of the 1930s and the heyday of *Mobo-Moga*.[1]

The low ceilings, narrow staircases and subtle decorations behind a façade covered with greenery have a special atmosphere, reflecting a certain pre-war refinement.

The building was designed by Kawamoto Ryoichi,[2] also responsible for the former military officers' club Kudan Kaikan and the now demolished (and sorely missed) Aoyama Dojunkai apartments at Omotesando, replaced by the Omotesando Hills complex. When it opened, the Okuno building had only six floors – the top floor is an extension. The residence is now home to a series of art galleries well-adapted to the ambience. Access is free and anyone can stroll up and down the narrow stairs and rather gloomy corridors. Don't miss the very unusual elevator, which has to be closed by hand with a folding metal grille, far from the sanitized and automated doors of modern mansions.

Next to the entrance you'll find a long explanation of how to use the elevator, which resembles those of some old Parisian apartment blocks. Adding to the retro feel, a needle indicates the floor.

NEARBY
Memorial to old Ginza ⑯

Not far from these memorials to old Ginza, near 1-11-2 (towards Kyobashi, below the expressway), is another souvenir of the past: a stele made from white brick notes that in the late 19th century the neighbourhood streets were of brick because of its fire-retardant qualities (see also p. 57). Next to the stele is a replica gas lamp.

Around eighty-five of these lamps illuminated the streets, and there are some reproductions at Ginza (notably next to the Apple Store). The combination of "white bricks and gas lamps" perfectly described the district at the end of the Meiji era. But the 1923 earthquake showed the limitations of brick construction.

A diorama of old Ginza can be seen in the Edo-Tokyo Museum at Ryogoku.

Yonei and Maruka buildings

At 2-8-20 Ginza, a few minutes' walk from the Okuno building, the Yonei building is another fine example of Western-style architecture in pre-war Ginza. It was completed in 1930. The façade of the upper floors, which is today uniform, was originally tiled and decorated in neoromantic style. The ground floor, with its arched windows, houses a posh pâtisserie and the upper floors serve as the offices of the Yonei company. The building is the work of Moriyama Matsunosuke,[3] designer of Japanese colonial architecture in Taiwan, including the Presidential Office in Taipei. Moriyama was also responsible for the Maruka building, dating from 1929, at 7-7-1 Ginza, which has plenty of personality but is a little less impressive than the Yonei.

---

[1] モボ・モガ, *abbreviation for Modern Boy, Modern Girl – Westernized youth culture and fashion of the 1920s and 30s.*
[2] 川元良一
[3] 森山松之介, *1869–1949.*

TSUKUDA PARK'S LIGHTHOUSE TOILETS

The "lighthouse" at the mouth of the river

1-11-4 Tsukuda, Chuo-ku (東京都中央区佃 1-11-4)
10-minute walk from Tsukishima station (月島), Tokyo metro Yurakucho line
Open 24/7

On the south side of Tsukuda Park, next to a pretty little Japanese garden, stands what appears to be an old-fashioned lighthouse.

The strange building is actually a monument over the public toilets, erected in memory of an actual lighthouse built in 1866 to guide vessels through the mouth of the Sumida.

This lighthouse, which no longer exists, was built by the magistrate in charge of the nearby Ishikawajima labour camp (石川島人足寄場 – see below).

Ishikawajima labour camp

In the late 18th century, Japan was afflicted by the Great Tenmei famine, one of the worst of the Edo period. Starvation led to a massive rural exodus and serious problems of unemployment, urban poverty and rampant crime. Following the ideas of Hasegawa Nobutame,[1] in 1790 the shogunate set up a labour camp at the mouth of the Sumida to rehabilitate the unemployed by teaching them the necessary skills and know-how to find a job. This was revolutionary for the times, which tended to favour a punitive approach – the shogunate didn't think twice about sending the unemployed down the mines.

[1] 長谷川宣以, 1745–1795, a hatamoto (samurai in the service of the shogunate), involved in fighting crime in Edo and the inspiration for much historical fiction, notably the series of novels adapted for TV as Onihei Hankacho (鬼平犯科帳).

NISHI-NAKA-DORI
NEIGHBOURHOOD WATCH POST

⑱

Oldest koban *in the country*

3-4-3 Tsukishima, Chuo-ku (東京都中央区月島 3-4-3)
5 minutes from Tsukishima station (月島), Tokyo metro Yurakucho line;
Toei subway Oedo line
Still in use

The building with the rather convoluted name of Nishi-Naka-dori neighbourhood watch post (⧠西仲通地域安全センター) was until 2007 the oldest *koban* in the country. Set up in 1921, it was originally a wooden shack before being replaced in 1926 by the small concrete building seen today, barely 5 metres long and painted maroon and cream.

The station, on Monja street, watches quietly over the *monjayaki* restaurants that bring Tsukishima most of its visitors.

Since becoming a neighbourhood watch post in 2007, it now houses "neighbourhood watch supporters" (地域安全サポーター), mostly former police officers. Lost visitors can ask them for directions; they'll also provide advice to deal with delinquency, and call the police if necessary.

Some Monja restaurants date back to the 1950s, but the concentration of restaurants in Tsukushima is quite a recent phenomenon. The Monja boom encouraged by the media in the late 80s, and the local publicity association set up at the end of the 90s with the support of Bulldog Sauce, put the district on the map, falsely giving it the air of a "traditional" gastronomic district. The task of energizing the district has clearly been a success: Nishi-Naka-dori is always bustling.

KACHIDOKI BRIDGE PYLON

An impressive mechanism

Museum: 6-20-11 Tsukiji, Chuo-ku (東京都中央区築地 6-20-11)
10-minute walk from Tsukiji station (築地), Tokyo metro Hibiya line
Open (museum): 9.30am–4.30pm (9am–4pm December and January)
Tuesday, Thursday, Friday and Saturday; closed 29 December to 3 January
Tours inside the bridge pylon: usually on Thursdays except public holidays,
in small groups and by reservation only (phone 03-5381-3380, Tokyo
Metropolitan Public Corporation for Road Improvement and Management)
Admission free

At the western end of the magnificent Kachidoki Bridge (勝鬨橋), next to the historic site of Tsukiji market, Kachidoki Bridge Museum (かちどき橋の資料館) is a tiny, usually deserted building that covers the history and structure of the double-leaf bascule bridge. You can also see the electric motors and control room.

You can book a tour inside the pylon housing the impressive mechanism that rotates up the bridge spans, but as it wasn't designed for tours expect a little discomfort.

The bridge was built in the 1940s as part of the city's major works projects to celebrate 2,600 years since Jimmu (legendary first emperor of Japan and founder of the imperial dynasty) ascended the throne. It hasn't been opened since the 1970s and the motors have had no power supply since 1980.

These major works also created a number of the city's amenities and great parks, such as Mizumoto, Kinuta and Shinozaki.

A bridge for Tokyo's 1940 Expo, the one that was never held

The Kachidoki Bridge led to the main site of the 1940 Grand International Exposition of Japan, also organized as part of celebrations of 2,600 years of the semi-legendary founding of the country, on reclaimed land on the waterfront of Harumi district. In the end, the Expo (poster on the right) was cancelled because of the Sino-Japanese War.

PASSAGE OF NISHI-GINZA JR CENTER

Oppressive shortcut between Yurakucho and Shinbashi

1-7 Uchisaiwaicho, Chiyoda-ku (東京都千代田区内幸町 1-7)
5-minute walk from Ginza station (銀座), Tokyo metro Ginza, Marunouchi or Hibiya linesMetro Marunouchi, Tokyo Metro Hibiya

The Nishi-Ginza JR Center (西銀座JRセンター) winds under a section of the Shinkansen tracks between Yurakucho and Shin-bashi. A gloomy passage runs across it for about 400 metres, so you can walk part of the distance between the two stations without getting soaked.

Built in the 1960s, before the opening of the Shinkansen high-speed network, the building is showing its age after a half-century of existence. Despite its very central location, this passage with its lugubrious atmos-phere is very little used as a shortcut.

Finding it isn't easy if you don't know where to look for the entrance, especially on the Shinbashi side, which is accessed through a car park with a low ceiling.

A rather lonely but authentic Korean restaurant towards the middle of the passage and a couple of bars liven up the evenings a little.

Highly specialized companies, some with links to JR Central, rent office space in this atypical environment, but much of the space seems to be unoccupied.

Just north of the passage, part of the area under the rails has been rehabilitated and restored for the opening in late 2010 of an old-style *yokocho*, *Sanchoku Inshokugai* (産直飲食街), bringing together several speciality *izakayas* (gastropubs). Despite its short history, the renovation has been astute enough to retain a very retro feel, with crates instead of seats, shared toilets and a narrow space to squeeze your way through. Whereas Nishi-Ginza JR Center is moribund, Sanchoku Inshokugai, a few metres away, is bursting with life.

NEARBY (21)
French door of Taimei municipal elementary school

Near Sanchoku Inshokugai, nestled just a short distance from the Su-kiyabashi and Yurakucho crossing, at 5-1-13 Ginza, the discreet Taimei municipal elementary school can boast of 140 years of history in the heart of one of Tokyo's most prestigious districts. Its main gate, on Miyuki-dori, is known as the "French door". If you can believe the plaque next to the door, it comes from the residence of an aristocratic family in the south of France.

The school was founded in 1878 and the current building dates from 1929, making Taimei one of the few schools to have survived from the city reconstruction plan following the Great Kanto Earthquake (although it was damaged during the war and later restored). The latest restoration, in 2014, has unfortunately got rid of the ivy that covered its walls. The school, however, has kept its refined air.

YURAKUCHO'S GODZILLA STATUE

The monster watches quietly

1-2-2 Yurakucho, Chiyoda-ku (東京都千代田区有楽町 1-2-2)
2-minute walk from Hibiya station (日比谷), Tokyo metro Chiyoda or Hibiya lines; Toei subway Mita line

I n front of the Hibiya Chanter shopping centre, a statue of Godzilla (ゴジラ像) was erected in 1995 to celebrate the 40th anniversary of the film. Not as imposing as the statue of the faithful dog Hachiko outside Shibuya station, this Godzilla is in a rather obscure corner so can't claim to be a landmark.

The little statue, which is undeservedly ignored by the crowds, is far from life-size but distinctly menacing.

Under the beast is a single disc, engraved with the perceptive quote, *Kono Gojira ha saigo no ippiki da to omoenai* (このゴジラが最後の一 匹だとは思えない – This Godzilla is probably not the last). In the same square, in the shadow of the monster, are handprints and signatures of various movie stars, mostly Japanese stars of Toho studios, although Tom Cruise and Jackie Chan have obviously also passed by.

NEARBY

Runic stone in Hibiya Park ㉓

Viking script commemorates polar route

In the heart of Hibiya Park, next to the pond of Shinji-ike in the northeast corner of the green space, is a remarkable runic stone engraved in Viking script.

The original was presented by Scandinavian Airlines in February 1967 to celebrate ten years since the opening of the Europe–Japan polar routes, and this is a replica.

On 24 February 1957, a DC-7 left Copenhagen. After a stopover in Anchorage, the aircraft reached Tokyo in just thirty-two hours.

At the same time, another DC-7 flew the route in the opposite direction. The opening of this new polar route has significantly reduced the journey time between Europe and Japan, which previously took around fifty hours. Next to the monument is a massive rock brought back from an expedition to Antarctica.

There are other diplomatic gifts in the park: a reproduction of Lupa Romana, the she-wolf suckling Romulus and Remus, presented in 1938 by the Italian Embassy; and a 1952 replica of the Liberty Bell from the United States.

FOX STATUES
OF TOYOKAWA-INARI TEMPLE

Get yourself promoted ...

1-4-7 Moto-Akasaka, Minato-ku (東京都港区元赤坂 1-4-7)
5 minutes from Akasaka-Mitsuke station (赤坂見附), Tokyo metro
Marunouchi, Ginza, Nagatacho (永田町), Nanboku, Hanzomon or Yurakucho
lines
Open daily 6am–8pm

A few steps from the bustle of Akasaka, the Toyokawa-Inari Buddhist temple (豊川稲荷東京別院) surprises visitors with the overwhelming number (and that's an understatement) of fox statues and statuettes. They're everywhere, in all shapes and sizes, in every corner. Here, a vixen and her cubs are revered by parents wanting their own children. There, at the rear of the temple, an octagonal stone is covered with offerings of statuettes of foxes – no surprises there – overlooked by a stack of other canines ...

The presence of these innumerable foxes is down to the cult of Dakini, a Buddhist protective temple deity, who traditionally rides a white fox. Toyokawa-Inari is the Tokyo branch of Toyokawa-Inari temple in Aichi prefecture, where there are even more fox statues.

In the temple grounds, a monumental stone stands over the tomb of its founder, Edo magistrate Oooka Tadasuke,[1] which could almost pass unnoticed among the foxes. Oooka, who came from a lowly background, had climbed the social ranks to become one of the most renowned city officials. This explains why the temple and its foxes are highly respected nowadays by anyone looking for promotion or success.

Dakini, Inari, Buddhism and Shinto

Goddess (among others) of crops and trade, Inari (稲荷神) is a Japanese deity of complex origin. Patron goddess of the Hata, a powerful clan that immigrated from China, she is celebrated in Fushimi-Inari shrine at Kyoto.

Inari is often identified with Ukanomitama (宇迦之御魂神), mentioned in the Kojiki (Records of Ancient Matters), and thus in fact part of the traditional Japanese Shinto pantheon. The fox, chasing pests that destroy crops, is her messenger animal. The syncretism between Buddhism and Shinto (神仏習合 – *Shinbutsu-shugo*) is perfectly represented by the rapprochement between Inari and Dakini, who were again divided in the Meiji era with the separation of the two religions. Both goddesses have however retained the same symbolism.

In the Meiji era, the temple had to prove its connection with Buddhism. Habit won and the temple kept its name, adding to the confusion. Toyokawa-Inari, celebrating Dakini not Inari, is a Buddhist not a Shinto temple.

---

[1] 大岡忠相, *1677–1752.*

MOUNT ATAGO STAIRWAY TO HEAVEN

The highest natural peak in the Yamanote hills

1-5-3 Atago, Minato-ku (東京都港区愛宕 1-5-3)
5-minute walk from Kamiyacho station (神谷町), Tokyo metro Hibiya line
Accessible 24/7

A short walk from Toranomon Hills skyscraper complex, Mount Atago (愛宕山) is officially the highest natural peak in the Yamanote hills. This peak with the Atago shrine perched on top of it rises 25.7 metres above sea level (or just over a tenth the height of Toranomon Hills...).

A flight of eighty steps up a 45-degree slope leads to the summit after a short but exhausting walk that almost feels like mountain-climbing. The view from the top, which was part of the famous views of the city 150 years ago, is now obstructed by the various buildings nearby.

There is however a photograph by Felice Beato,[1] taken from the top of the steps a few years before the Meiji Restoration, one of the rare panoramas of Edo.

Walking up the steps is a minor personal challenge, even for athletes. For the record, only four riders have managed to reach the summit on horseback. The first was Magaki Heikuro,[2] of the Marugame clan of Sanuki, in 1634, to the surprise of the 3rd Tokugawa shogun, who had challenged his riders to fetch a plum-tree branch from the top. The feat was repeated in 1882 and again in 1925. The most recent horseback climber was a television stuntman in 1982. Tables of these exploits are on display in the shrine.

Although higher, Hakone-Yama (see p. 164) is an artificial hill.

NEARBY
NHK Museum of Broadcasting ㉖
Origins of the telly

The main ancestor of NHK, Tokyo Broadcasting Corporation (known by its call-signal JOAK) broadcast radio from the heights of Mount Atago from July 1925 to 1938. In 1956, NHK opened the world's first museum dedicated to TV and radio broadcasting on the premises of the JBC. The present building dates from 1968. The museum is free, and quite remarkable for anyone interested in the history of broadcasting. The four densely packed floors display early cameras, the first experimental TV systems (still working), vinyl records used during the war, examples of the first studio sets, costumes, etc.

---

[1] *1832–1909. British photographer born in Italy. Beato moved to Yokohama in 1863, and took his priceless photographs of Japan towards the end of the Edo period.*
[2] 曲垣平九郎, ?–?

FORMER OMOTESANDO PLATFORMS ON THE GINZA LINE

Changes at the station

3-6-12 Kita-Aoyama, Minato-ku (東京都港区北青山 3-6-12)
Omotesando station (表参道), Tokyo metro Ginza, Chiyoda or Hanzomon lines
Inaccessible to the public but partly visible from platforms of Ginza and Hanzomon lines

The old platforms of Omotesando station on the Ginza line are closed to the public but can still be seen, either from the end of the modern Omotesando platforms looking towards Shibuya, or through the window of the Ginza subway just before arriving in Omotesando (or just after, depending on the direction ...).

The old platforms are not usually lit up, but the light from the station may be enough to make out their tiled walls and even a few signs. If you're a passenger, the train runs very slowly at this point, allowing a clear view of what's left of them.

Omotesando station on the Ginza line has changed its name several times, and even its site. Originally opened in 1938 under the name of Aoyama Rokuchome, the station was renamed the following year in Jingumae. In 1972 the station changed its name at last to Omotesando, on the opening of the Chiyoda line station, where you can now make

a complicated transfer that even involves going outside.

The latest change came in 1978 at the opening of the Hanzomon line: the original platforms of the Ginza line were permanently closed to the public and the trains stop a little to the north-east, sharing the Hanzomon platforms.

Tokyo stations are moving with the times, literally...

"TOUCHABLE" EXHIBITION ROOM ㉘ MINATO CITY LOCAL HISTORY MUSEUM

Feel the whalebone

5-28-4 Shiba, Minato-ku (東京都港区芝 5-28-4)
2-minute walk from Mita station (三田), Toei subway Asakusa or Mita lines;
5 minutes from Tamachi station (田町), JR Yamanote line
Open 9am–5pm, closed Sundays and public holidays (except July and August)
and the third Thursday of the month – if Thursday is a public holiday the
museum is open, but closed the following day; closed December 28 to January 4
Admission free

Minato City Local History Museum (港区立郷土資料館), on the fourth floor of the municipal library, has some interesting permanent exhibitions of local history. These include finds from archaeological excavations in shell middens, when several thousand artefacts of all kinds from the Jomon period were recovered. The museum's most innovative feature is its touchable exhibition room. Whereas most of the world's museums do their utmost to conserve their exhibits, the Minato Museum unequivocally encourages visitors to run their fingers over a complete minke whale skeleton and the skulls of common animals (dogs, cats, cows...). You're even allowed to examine and feel pottery from the Jomon, Yayoi and Kofun periods, as well as some more recent objects that younger generations will have probably never handled (treadle sewing machine, cold-storage ice chamber, charcoal-burning and gas irons, coal brazier, etc.).

Archaeological excavations in the shell middens took place in 1978 near Mitadai Park at 4-17-28 Mita. Several permanent exhibitions on the excavations and a replica of a prehistoric cave dwelling are kept in this park. The figurines holding explanatory notices are rather unusual.

TAKANAWA CENTRAL PASSAGE

Taxi nightmare

Between Shibaura Minato-ku and Konan Minato-ku
(東京都港区芝浦~港区港南)
5-minute walk from Sengakuji station (泉岳寺), Toei subway Asakusa
and Keikyu Honsen lines
Accessible 24/7

Takanawa Central Passage (高輪中央架道橋), a narrow one-way tunnel under the Yamanote line north of Shinagawa station, surely deserves the nickname "sign killer" (提灯殺し) that some Tokyo taxi drivers have given it.

With a height restriction of 1.5 metres, this claustrophobic nightmare of a tunnel is too low to negotiate without scratching the signs on the roof of some private taxis, not to mention cars, which are often higher than the taxis.

The tunnel also has a rather narrow footpath: with a ceiling height seemingly less than 170 centimetres, the tallest pedestrians need to duck to avoid banging their heads.

For pedestrians, the speed of the cars and the height of the roof make the 250-metre tunnel impressive at the very least, provided they don't meet any traffic. Cycling through it is a real adventure.

Despite the extensive housing developments planned nearby with the opening of a new station on the Yamanote line, Central Passage should survive.

> Today, the vast majority of cars venturing into the tunnel are taxis whose drivers know the way and take a mischievous pleasure in putting their foot down to scare their passengers.

NEARBY

Arimasutonbiru house ㉚

4-15-35 Mita, Minato-ku (東京都港区三田 4-15-35)
10-minute walk from Tamachi station (田町), JR Yamanote or Keihin-Tohoku lines
Accessible 24/7

A short distance from Keio University's Mita campus, Oka Keisuke,[1] an architect with first-class qualifications, has, since 2005, been almost singlehandedly building the house of his dreams on a plot he acquired in 2000. The house, named *Arimasutonbiru* (蟻鱒鳶ル – Ant-Trout-Kite[2] Building, the three animals representing earth, water and sky depicted on a green panel upstairs), is in a potential urban redevelopment area. But Keisuke, dubbed the Gaudí of Mita, is battling to be able to finish his work.

Although the house is unfinished and will still probably take him a few years, it's obvious that good progress is being made on a particularly unusual construction, which could be described as a three-storey concrete realization of a cubist painting.

What you can already see is surprising enough: the window openings are deliberately irregular, the finished walls are anything but flat and smooth, and sometimes richly decorated. Through the openings a highly unusual concrete interior can be glimpsed.

For those who care about complying with the law, don't worry: the plans have been certified and a building permit issued, so the work isn't the disaster zone of an enlightened eccentric but the road to a maverick's dream.

---

[1] 岡啓輔, 1965–.
[2] *Incidentally a play on words, as* arimasu *means "existing".*

SEISHIN JOSHI GAKUIN SCHOOL GATEWAY

Tokyo's only example of German Art Nouveau architecture

4-11-1 Shirokane, Minato-ku (東京都港区白金 4-11-1) • 10 minutes from Shirokanedai station (白金台), Tokyo metro Nanboku line; Toei subway Mita line

The main gateway of Seishin Joshi Gakuin school (聖心女学院), erected in 1909, is the only architectural example of German Art Nouveau (*Jugendstil*) in Tokyo. This is actually a vestige from the original campus, destroyed in the 1923 earthquake, a lost work by Czech architect Jan Letzel[1].

Originally located a little farther away, at the top of the hill, the gateway was moved in 1935 and the bricks replaced with a reinforced concrete structure. Particularly noteworthy are the meticulous carvings of turtles (significance a mystery) on the sides of the gateway, and the heart surrounded by thorns over the archway, a symbol of the Sacred Heart. The wooden gates have a far more Japanese look, the mix of two styles adding to the personality of the gateway.

The main building of the school campus, dating from 1928, is by Antonin Raymond. Not usually open to the public.

Jan Letzel was also the architect of the Hiroshima Prefectural Industrial Promotion Hall, built in 1915, and the infamous Atomic Bomb Dome or Hiroshima Peace Memorial, now a UNESCO World Heritage site.

Antonin Raymond, initiator of Japanese modernist architecture

Raymond, born in Bohemia (Czech Republic) in 1888, is considered one of the initiators of Japanese modernist architecture and has influenced leading architects such as Kenzo Tange (see also p. 225). He came to Japan in 1919 as assistant to Frank Lloyd Wright[2] on the Hotel Imperial project and in 1922 his own office won acclaim with its work for Tonjo. In the 1920s and 30s, Raymond participated in numerous projects (such as Seishin University) where concrete was the main building material. He left Japan in 1938, then returned in 1947 and took part in the reconstruction effort, with many achievements in the 1950s and 70s throughout the country, such as St Alban's Church in Minato ward and Raymond Hall in Mie prefecture. He died in 1976, but the Raymond Architectural Design Office is still in business.

---

[1] *1880-1925.*
[2] *1867-1959. American architect.*

REMAINS OF ODAIBA CANNON BATTERIES

Edo defences

Site of the third battery: 1-10-1 Daiba, Minato-ku (東京都港区台場 1-10-1)
10-minute walk from Odaiba-Kaihin-koen station (お台場海浜公園),
Yurikamome line

Τhe arrival of Perry's ships in 1853 to demand the opening up of the country had an immediate effect on the city. The shogunate, which was worried about the risk of an attack on Edo by sea, rapidly ordered the construction of eleven six- and five-sided batteries of cannons in the bay and one on the banks, two months after the arrival of the "Black Ships". Eight of these were partially or fully completed in just a few months. Four have since been covered by the expansion of the city in the waters of the bay or demolished to make way for shipping. The remains of four of them are more or less integrated into the urban fabric, hence the name of the well-known boulevard of Odaiba (お 台 場 – *Odaiba,* battery).

The structure of the third battery (第三台場), the best known, is still easily accessible from the tip of Odaiba. The site was converted in 1928 to create Daiba Park. A crucible and the remains of a powder warehouse are still there while the guns on display are reproductions.

The sixth and best-preserved battery (第六台場) is clearly visible in the waters of the bay about 300 metres from the third battery: the "mystery island" next to the Rainbow Bridge. Unfortunately public access is totally prohibited. You can spot the berth from the bridge.

There are also some vestiges of the fourth battery (第四台場), which was never completed. The structure, originally an island, was absorbed into the Tennozu boulevard. The pedestrian walk along the waterfront by the Daiichi Hotel Tokyo Seafort has reused its stone walls.

The Goten Miyashita battery (御殿山下台場) was located next to the mouth of the Megurogawa near the Shinagawa *shukuba* (see p. 61). The well-appointed Daiba municipal elementary school (品川区立台 場小学校 – Shinagawa Battery municipal elementary school) now occupies the site. The silhouette of the battery is easily located on a map. In front of the school is a copy of the lighthouse that used to stand on the second battery.

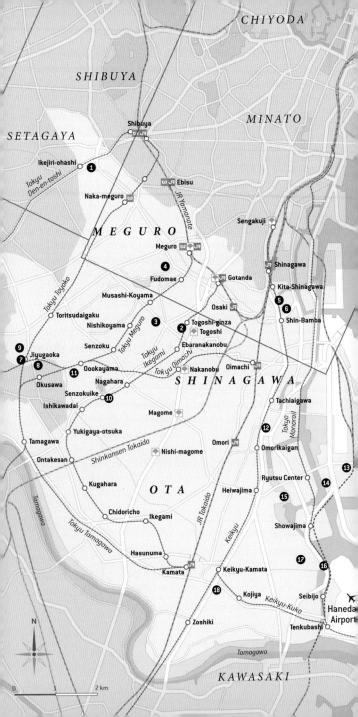

Ota / Shinagawa / Meguro

MEGURO SKY GARDEN

Hanging gardens

1-9-2 Ohashi, Meguro-ku (東京都目黒区大橋 1-9-2)
3-minute walk from Ikejiri Ohashi station (池尻大橋), Tokyu Den-en-Toshi line
Open 7am–9pm daily

Anord North of Sangenjaya, Route 3 of the urban expressway joins the Central Circular Route (C2), here underground, at the impressive Ohashi interchange right next to Ikejiri Ohashi station. Lack of space means that the expressway disappears into the bowels of the city to join Route C2 via a spiral structure on four levels. The roof of this spiral is covered by the amazing Meguro Sky Garden (目黒天空庭園), opened in March 2013.

This pleasant aerial park consists of a 400-metre strip of greenery, inclined and curved, following the slope of the route it covers. Its lowest point is 11 metres above ground level, its highest 35 metres, making it one of the few parks that can only be reached by elevator.

The entrance to the elevator to the lower section is near the post office along Route 246.

Up in the hanging gardens, there's a fine unobstructed view of Tokyo from an unusual angle.

The upper garden is connected to ground level via the lobby on the 9th floor of Cross Air Tower, a massive residential block that forms part of the structure covering the interchange.

WHITE-BRICK MEMORIAL OF TOGOSHI-GINZA

②

First Ginza outside Chuo

2-17-10 Hiratsuka, Shinagawa-ku (東京都品川区平塚 2-17-10)
5 minutes from Togoshi-Ginza station (戸越銀座), Tokyu Ikegami line;
or 5 minutes from Togoshi station (戸越), Toei subway Asakusa line

I n the depths of Shinagawa, the pedestrian shopping street of Togoshi-Ginza (戸越銀座), which is really three separate streets leading in to each other, is Tokyo's longest at 1,300 metres.

It's no coincidence that the street is known as "Ginza", after the famous area of Chuo ward.

After the 1923 earthquake, the white bricks from the other Ginza, severely damaged by the disaster, were recovered by Togoshi traders to pave their own street, which finally opened in 1927 as *Togoe* (戸越).

Not far from the station, towards 2-17-10 Hiratsuka, a commemorative stone inscribed *Togoshi to Ginza yukari no Hi* (戸越と銀座ゆかりの碑 – Stele of the Connection between Ginza and Togoshi) sits on top of two of these old bricks in a glass case to evoke the origins of the district. These bricks, with their *romanized* "SHINAGAWA" stamp, are from a factory founded in 1875 that became the Shinagawa brickyard in 1887.

NEARBY
PALM

③

The longest covered arcade in the city

Far from Chuo's fashion boutiques and jewellers, Togoshi-Ginza has rows of little local shops and family restaurants in low buildings. Togoshi also presents itself as one of Tokyo's *korokke* (croquettes) high spots. Nearby, the Musashi-Koyama shopping arcade (aka PALM) is the longest in the city.

STATUES OF GOHYAKU RAKAN-JI

300 statues in a temple dedicated to 500

3-20-11 Shimomeguro, Meguro-ku (東京都目黒区下目黒 3-20-11)
10-minute walk from Fudomae station (不動前), Tokyu Meguro line
Open 9am–5pm daily

Of the 500 or so statuettes created in the late 17th century by the monk-sculptor Shouun Genkei,[1] Gohyaku Rakan-ji (五百羅漢寺 – Temple of 500 Rakan) still has exactly 305 of these wooden statues of Buddhist disciples, including 287 seated.

The temple with its statues was originally sited in the old district of Honjo at Ojima, in what is now Koto ward. Although the temple experienced some high points during the shogunate, such as being depicted in the *ukiyo-e* of Utagawa and Hokusai, it also had some lows, gradually falling into disuse in the Meiji era. It was moved here in late 1908 and almost abandoned until the arrival of Okoi, the geisha who became a nun (see below). The present buildings date from the 1980s. The *rakan* statuettes are displayed in the *Rakando* (羅漢堂) and the *Hondo*. Inspired by the stone statuettes in Rakan-ji at Honyabakei in what is now Oita prefecture, the monk Shouun made his own *rakan* from the age of 44, when he came to Edo. This collection of his statuettes with their various poses and expressions, all less than a metre high, form an astonishing and too rarely visited display.

Okoi

Okoi (お鯉), real name Ando Teruko (安藤照子), was born in Yotsuya in 1880. At the age of 14 she joined the world of flowers and willows, becoming one of the geisha at Shinbashi *kagai*. After a short failed marriage with a *Kabuki* actor, she returned to Shinbashi. Renowned for her beauty and intelligence, Okoi developed links with leading politicians of the Meiji era. Yamagata Aritomo (see p. 226) presented her to prime minister Katsura Taro,[2] who was impressed by her strong character, and she even became his mistress. After some trouble with the law, in 1938 she became a nun and priestess of Rakanji. She died in 1948. A statue of Kannon dedicated to her stands in the temple next to the *hondo*.

---

[1] 松雲元慶, *1648–1710*.
[2] 桂太郎, *1848–1913. Imperial army general in the Meiji Restoration, governor-general of Taiwan, three times prime minister and holder of various ministerial posts in the early 20th century.*

WHALE BURIED AT KAGATA SHRINE ⑤

Grounded in Edo Bay

1-7-17 Higashi-Shinagawa, Shinagawa-ku (東京都品川区東品川 1-7-17)
5-minute walk from Kita-Shinagawa station (北品川), Keikyu Honsen line
Accessible 24/7

In front of Kagata shrine (利田神社), dedicated to the Buddhist deity Benzaiten, you might well be surprised to come across a little statue of a whale seeming to leap from the sidewalk, as well as a whale-shaped swing for children.

They commemorate the remains of a whale buried under a small mound at the shrine.

In 1798, the 18-metre whale drifted into Edo Bay. Local fishermen eventually captured it by driving it ashore.

Here was great excitement among the local residents, fascinated by a creature such as they'd never seen before. Rumours of the whale's presence spread like wildfire around Edo and even reached the ears of the 11th shogun, Tokugawa Ienari,[1] who asked to see it.

The carcass was towed a few kilometres to Hamarikyu to comply with Ienari's request. In the end it was butchered, but most of the skeleton is buried at Kagata shrine.

Shinagawaura: the old mouth of the Megurogawa

Right next to the shrine is a small stretch of water running slightly inland. This is the old fishing port of Shinagawaura (品川浦), which lay at the mouth of the Meguro River until it was diverted just before the war.

NEARBY
Shinagawa-shuku   ⑥
Remains of southern Edo

Shinagawaura and Kagata shrine were near the shores of Edo Bay, next to the *shukuba* (see p. 155). At that time, this was the real economic centre of Shinagawa, rather than the area around the modern station of the same name.

The fact that Shinagawa station, the country's first (opened 1872), is in Minato rather than Shinagawa is one of those small geographical curiosities everyone is familiar with but not many know why.

Shinagawa-shuku *shukuba* was the first stop on the Tokaido route to Kyoto, the most important of the Five Routes of the Edo period leading in and out of the capital. Conflicts of interest between the *shukuba* merchants in the Meiji era moved the site of the new railway station a little to the north. Over the years, boundary changes finally left the station outside Shinagawa ward and the *shukuba* soon lost its importance as it was too far from the trains, ironically enough.

Shinagawa-shuku stretched roughly from the east of Kita-Shinagawa station to road 421 near Aomono-Yokocho station. All that remains of the southern gate of the capital is a shopping street, animated enough but far from being a hub of activity. There are a few stones commemorating historical sites and a certain ambience of a glorious but distant past. The inn at the heart of the *shukuba*, the *honjin*, was located in Seiseki Park at 2-7-21 Kita-Shinagawa. Not far from Kita-Shinagawa station, at the entrance to the *shukuba* near the Yotsuyamai Bridge (where Godzilla came ashore in the 1954 film), a non-profit organization has opened a small but lively tourist centre dedicated to the fascinating history of *shukuba* at 1-2-6 Kita-Shinagawa (open 10am–4pm at weekends and on public holidays). You can find a stack of information there on the neighbourhood as well as detailed maps of the main sites. English-speaking guides are sometimes available.

---

[1] 徳川家斉, *1773–1841, shogun from 1787 to 1837.*

TORII OF THE TOYOKAWA-INARI AT JIYUGAOKA

A torii without a shrine

1-29 Jiyugaoka, Meguro-ku (東京都目黒区自由が丘 1-29)
5 minutes from Jiyugaoka station (自由が丘), Tokyu Toyoko or Oimachi lines
Accessible 24/7

Just north of Jiyugaoka station concourse, an isolated red *torii* bearing the inscription *Toyokawa-Inari Daimyojin* (豊川稲荷大明神) stands rather mysteriously in the middle of a narrow pedestrian street.

Its presence is all the more unexpected as no shrine can be seen nearby. In addition, the street is not very crowded, and is nothing like a *sando*.

The Toyokawa-Inari of Jiyugaoka is actually a *bunrei* of Toyokawa-Inari of Akasaka (see p. 42), so constitutes the remains of a religious site on the borderline between Buddhism and Shinto. A Shinto *hokora* shrine was removed in 2008 during the demolition of a nearby building, leaving only the *torii*, stuck in the alley.

In the mid-1930s, when the city was taking root around Jiyugaoka, a religious site had been "invited" to come to the area, to ensure the commercial success of the small businesses and shops that were springing up.

Until 1958, the area around the station was animated every 1st, 11th and 21st of the month by a market around 150 stalls, watched over by the Toyokawa-Inari.

NEARBY
Naval village
8

Officers' homes from the 1920s

In the early 1920s, a landowner in what is today Okuzawa district sealed a contract with the Navy Ministry to develop the area to house high-ranking officers, as it was ideally situated between the ministry and the military port of Yokosuka.

This is how in the 1930s, a good thirty officers' homes were established here; the upmarket residences had gardens filled with palms.

Three beautiful houses (private, so not visitable, but can be seen from the street) have survived at 2-33 Okuzawa (at numbers 2, 15 and 16), about 500 metres east of Jiyugaoka station in Setagaya.

A Venetian canal in Tokyo
9

The Kuhonbutsu River, tributary of the Tamagawa, has since the mid-1970s flowed south-east of Jiyugaoka, buried under the asphalt of the green corridor of Kuhonbut-sugawa Ryokudo.

Picture yourself for a moment in Paris, Rome or New York, seated on a bench on a cobbled street, sipping a coffee.

On the other side of the station, towards 2-8-3 Jiyuogaoka, is a small replica of a Venetian canal right in the centre of La Vita shopping complex.

Crouching under the rails

2-30 Kami-Ikedai, Ota-ku (東京都大田区上池台 2-30)
2-minute walk from Senzoku-Ike station (洗足池), Tokyu Ikegami line
Accessible 24/7

Right next to the car park alongside the Mos Burger at the north exit of Senzoku-Ike station, opposite Nakahara Kaido avenue, there is a pedestrian passage, not exactly a tunnel, where you can plunge under the rails of the Tokyu Ikegami line.

The passage is extremely low, to the point that an adult has to crouch down, and it's probably impossible to cycle through. It lies directly under the track, so when the trains trundle overhead you get a rather frightening unrestricted view. Just by raising a hand you could touch the railway sleepers... although that's probably not a good idea.

NEARBY
Tokodai blossom ⑪
Cherry trees at the university

A few minutes' walk from Senzoku-Ike pond will take you to the main campus of the Tokyo Institute of Technology (東京工業大学), aka Tokodai, at Ooookayama.

Remember that Ooookayama is spelled with three "o"s when correctly romanized. The institute was originally in Taito ward but moved here in 1924 after the campus was severely damaged in the 1923 earthquake.

The central building (本館 – *honkan*), completed in 1934, survived the war. In front of this building, some stunning cherry trees bloom in spring, a sight not to be missed by anyone who enjoys the blossoms but wants to avoid the dense crowds in the centre of Tokyo. The campus also opens its doors to the public during the Hanami (literally "Flower Viewing") festival to allow everyone to enjoy the cherry blossom. (Note that alcohol is officially banned.)

REMAINS OF SUZUGAMORI EXECUTION SITE

Beheadings in the south of the city

2-5-6 Minami-Oi, Shinagawa-ku (東京都品川区南大井 2-5-6)
10-minute walk from Omori-Kaigan station (大森海岸), Keikyu line

Another vast Edo execution site, along with Kozukappara (see p. 270), Suzugamori (鈴ヶ森刑場) has also seen many heads roll. Although there are no detailed records, between 100,000 and 200,000 executions are alleged to have occurred during its busiest period between 1651 and 1871.

The site was located at the southern entrance to the city on the Tokaido route, before arriving at the Shinagawa *shukuba* (see p. 61). It acted as a warning to anyone thinking of committing a crime in the capital. You can once again take stock here of the extent of the city built on reclaimed land, as the site used to be just beside the sea.

The field is nowadays a picturesque area, peaceful and forgotten along the Daiichi Keihin highway that has replaced the Tokaido. There are several interesting remains of the various methods of execution among the trees, however. A stand for a stake can still be seen, as well as a base to support a crucifixion cross (legs apart). A basin, now covered with wire mesh, was used to wash the decapitated heads. There are other stelae and offerings for more natural deaths.

Several notorious personalities have lived out their last moments at Suzugamori: Marubashi Chuya,[1] *ronin* instigator of the Keian rebellion,[2] who is said to be the first to have been executed at Suzugamori in 1651; the outlaw Hirai Gonpachi,[3] represented in several *ukiyo-e* and executed in 1679; and Yaoya Oshichi,[4] who started a fire so she could meet with her lover; the fire spread and destroyed a large section of downtown Edo. Oshichi has been the source of inspiration for a great deal of fiction and was burned at the stake at the age of 16 (although even his historical existence is disputed).

You can visit the criminology section of Meiji University Museum (see p. 16) to learn more about the various methods of execution, which were far from being quick and painless.

The battlefield on which the heads of criminals were exposed to the public.

[1] 丸橋忠弥, ?–1651.
[2] 慶安の変, *failed coup against the shogunate in 1651 by a group of* ronin *(samurai with no lord or master), very indicative of an underlying problem about what to do with the warriors in peaceful Edo: this encouraged the shogunate to promote reforms to help them find work.*
[3] 平井権八, 1655–1679.
[4] 八百屋お七, 1668–1683.

WILD BIRD PARK AT TOKYO PORT

A nature sanctuary alongside the track

3-1 Tokai, Ota-ku (東京都大田区東海 3-1)
25-minute walk from Ryutsu Center station (物流センター), Monorail line;
or 5 minutes from Tokyoko Yacho-koen bus stop (東京港野鳥公園); Keikyu
line 森43 from JR Omori
Open 9am–5pm February to October, 9am–4.30pm November to January,
every day except Monday – if a public holiday falls on a Monday the park
is open, but closed the following day; closed for year-end holidays

Not far from the runways of Haneda Airport, the wild bird park in Tokyo Port (東京港野鳥公園) makes an unlikely but relaxing bird sanctuary along the bay.

As there's no direct public transport from the city centre, you could easily find yourself virtually alone, even at weekends, watching the dozens of wild bird species seeking refuge in the swamps, under the roar of jets taking off.

The 25-hectare park was created on land reclaimed from the sea. Numerous birds were already visiting the new terrain while the site was under construction, attracted by the stretches of water that collected there, and it soon became popular with birdwatchers.

The park, opened by Tokyo Metropolitan Government in 1978 and extended in 1989, is now one of the country's nine wild bird sanctuaries directly managed by the *Wild Bird Society of Japan*.

Visitors are restricted to paths interspersed with four raised observation areas, where telescopes are available for anyone without their own binoculars.

At the foot of the small exhibition centre on the east side, an outdoor track has been laid so you can look out for the crabs and other small creatures that live in the wetlands.

On the whole, the park is a successful example of a small patch of urban land totally restored to nature, which has effectively taken over, a sort of apologetic gift from Tokyo for all the disturbance...

Sweet-smelling auction

2-2 Tokai, Ota-ku (東京都大田区東海 2-2)
15-minute walk from Ryutsu Center station (物流センター), Monorail line
Open to visitors 5am–3pm, closed Sunday
Flower-section auction at 7am, occasionally closed

Ota market has a flower section (大田市場花き部) of over 2 hectares, in a large hall crowned by a floral statue, separated from the other halls by the Wangan stretch of the urban expressway.

This flower market may not be as vast as the one at Aalsmeer in the Netherlands, but the morning auction, the largest in the country, has the virtue of being at an almost reasonable hour compared with Tsukiji (from 7am anyway). Definitely a worthwhile spectacle.

About 3 million flowers are sold daily, a good third of all the sales in Japan. Little windows let visitors watch the auction without disturbing anyone (only accredited professionals can participate).

Dozens of buyers all sit around in a large amphitheatre that wouldn't look out of place in a university, with everybody bidding from a special electronic device.

Unlike many auctions of fresh produce, Ota market flowers are priced on a sliding scale – the price of lots in the lower area of the amphitheatre comes up on large central displays, and decreases until a buyer makes a bid.

Ota, a vast but accessible market

You can easily visit Ota market (the largest in the city after Toyosu). In the general halls, a tour itinerary is marked out on the ground with explanatory signs at points of interest.

The route follows a raised walkway to avoid interfering with market operations while enjoying some of the bustle. It also offers a superlative view of Mount Fuji as well as the small figureheads symbolizing the products sold.

The tour's starting point is almost hidden on the second floor of the administration building, on the south side.

Auctions in the main halls are held at 5.40am for seafood and 6.50am for fruit and vegetables.

The goods bought by each wholesaler are then offered for sale to distributors and other traders in the halls.

The general public is not allowed to purchase fresh produce in the auction halls but you can shop in the annex (関連棟) between the fruit/veg and the seafood halls.

OMORI NORI MUSEUM

The best seaweed came from the bay

2-2 Heiwanomori-koen, Ota-ku (東京都大田区平和の森公園 2-2)
10-minute walk from Heiwajima station (平和島), Keikyu Honsen line
Open 9am–5pm daily, 9am–7pm June to August, daily except on the third
Monday of the month – if a public holiday falls on a Monday the museum
is open, but closed the following day; closed 29 December to 3 January

Omori Nori Museum (大森海苔のふるさと館), in Heiwa no Mori Park, is free and not much visited.

It is devoted to seaweed production, documenting what used to be the main local industry.

The Ota coasts had been known for the quality of their seaweed since the Edo period, and even until after the war, before the roadworks of the early 1960s forced farms to close down.

At the time, much of Haneda Airport was also built on reclaimed algae culture basins.

Two harvesting boats are displayed on the ground floor of the museum. The second floor has a series of specialized tools and numerous period photographs and information boards explaining the methods used.

Don't miss trying on the fishermen's *getas*, high sandals weighed down by stones that the seaweed gatherers used to move around in the silt. You can also get onto the roof for an ideal view of Omori Furusato no Hamabe Park's pleasant beach, packed with families enjoying themselves in summer.

For gourmets hungry after their museum visit, the seaweed industry hasn't completely disappeared, although production is no longer local. There are still several retailers and wholesalers in the area. You'll find some speciality shops in the streets around Sangyo-dori and east of Heiwajima station.

HANEDA MOVABLE BRIDGE

A road into space

View from the riverbank at 5-2 Omori-Minami, Ota-ku (東京都大森南 5-2)
25-minute walk from Amamori-Inari station (穴守稲荷), Keihin-Kyuko Kuko
line
Accessible 24/7

South of Morigasaki Park, the narrow footpath along the banks of the Nomigawa near Omori Junior High School offers a perfect view of the Haneda movable bridge (羽田可動橋).

This ingenious bridge dating from 1994 has two pivoting sections that were only in use for four years.

The bridge was built to relieve traffic congestion in the parallel tunnel while allowing for overhead height constraints (proximity to the

airport) and clearance for river traffic. The diversion proved unnecessary, however, with the gradual extension of the Wangan expressway that relieved National Route 1.

Although the bridge has been left open since 1998, it's in working order and technically could be used again one day...

Morigasaki Park: on the roof of a waste recycling centre

North of the mouth of the Nomigawa, in a former spa that had several *ryokan* (traditional guest houses) before the war, Morigasaki Park (森ヶ崎公園) is little used even at weekends. This "dead zone" of Tokyo is rather poorly served by rail.

The nearest station, Anamori-Inari, is over 20 minutes walk away. The park is actually laid out on the roof of the eastern zone of Morigasaki recycling centre.

The western part is on the artificial island of Showajima. The centre, the largest in the country, was opened in 1967 on the site of a fish factory.

The park, with its tennis courts, children's games and observation towers offering unbeatable views of the planes at Haneda Airport, can be identified by the open-air water tanks of the recycling facility. The stench of the garbage doesn't seem to bother the admittedly rare visitors who venture down here.

NEARBY

Jizo at Hojoin temple ⑰
Memories of a pre-war disaster

A modest statue of Jizo (Buddhist protector of children) in the garden of the small Hojoin temple at 5-1-18 Minami-Oomori is dedicated to one of the country's worst pre-war air disasters. On the morning of 24 August 1938, a Fokker cargo plane and a Hanriot fighter collided above the neighbourhood. The Fokker crashed into a factory (near Omori Fourth Elementary School), the other plane hit a house near the shore. Only five crew members were on board the two planes, but the Fokker tank exploded on the ground and another eighty-five people perished in the fire.

PIO

Industrial site welcomes visitors

1-20-20 Minami-Kamata, Ota-ku (東京都大田区南蒲田 1-20-20)
2-minute walk from Keikyu-Kamata station (京急鎌田), Keikyu Honsen
or Keikyu Kuko lines
Open 9am–5pm weekdays, 10am–5pm Saturdays, closed Sundays and public
holidays and 29 December to 3 January

The best place to get the measure of the industrial side of Ota ward is the fantastically futuristic Ota City Industrial Promotion Organization complex, aka PiO (大田区産業プラザ・PiO).

It houses meeting and exhibition venues aimed at the multiple local workshops and small factories 100 metres south of Keikyu-Kamata station.

The visitor information point is upstairs.

Maps show the workshops and factories open to the public and there is information on the neighbourhood's distinctive industrial nature.

The centre also has a café and restaurant.

Shitamachi bobsled

The Ota City Industrial Promotion Organization seems to be trying its best to salvage the industrial and craft heritage of Ota.

For example, the Shitamachi bobsled project initiated in 2011 aims to develop a "made-in-Ota" bobsled, an ambitious goal given that the sport is almost non-existent in Japan. A few dozen small factories around PiO helped to develop the first model.

The sled took part in the March 2013 America's Cup Bobsled at Lake Placid in the United States, finishing seventh out of eleven and becoming the first Japanese sled to compete in an international race. The dream didn't stop there as the Jamaican team, another newcomer to this sport, has decided to use the Shitamachi bobsled in the 2018 Pyeongchang Winter Olympics.

Background: Ota or urban deindustrialization

The Ota ward sees itself as the pinnacle of the Japanese precision industries, the mecca of *monozukuri* (craft production).

Without Ota there'd be no rockets, they say; without Ota, no DVD players. Even the first Microsoft mouse of the 1980s was made in Ota …

There are enough small factories and industrial workshops with fewer than ten employees concentrated in the area to make the Adachi ward green with envy, although their number is diminishing year by year.

Over half of them have fewer than three employees. Today there are about 4,000 workshops, while there was more than double that number in their 1980s heyday.

The term "deindustrialization" often brings to mind vast suburban factories abruptly closing down to the dismay of thousands of workers, leaving their region in turmoil.

The deindustrialization of Ota is more subtle and gradual. Even though thousands of jobs have been lost with the closure of small workshops, the ward isn't exactly plagued by unemployment and poverty, although the exclusive garden suburb of Den-en-Chofu skews the statistics.

The local speciality is metallurgy, in which 80 per cent of the workshops and factories produce and assemble precision parts (often only one, as it happens) for sale to industrial manufacturers. Increased competition from abroad requires these small workshops to concentrate on quality, proximity and flexibility, with stocks that can be adapted to requirements in a 10-minute cycle trip. Working in an urban environment, it is of course impossible to rely on price wars alone.

The heart of industrial Ota lies south and east of Kamata, in the streets of the Kojiya, Haneda, Omori and Rokugo neighbourhoods, north and south of the last stretch of the Nomigawa.

The workshops blend harmoniously with ageing houses and small apartments.

Along the major roads, large mansions are beginning to appear. This is the deindustrialization of Ota: small local industries disappear to the benefit of the rest of the city.

Signs on the frontage of the noisiest workshops ask residents for their understanding with the aim of peaceful coexistence.

The rows of workshops, animated during the week, are deserted at weekends, but you can identify them even when closed from the licences posted outside.

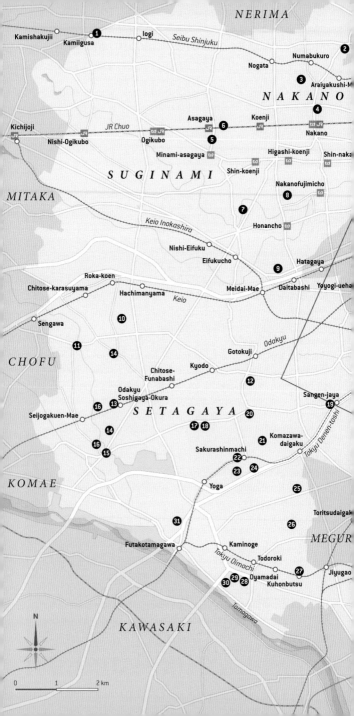

NERIMA

Kamishakujii
Kamiigusa ❶
Iogi
Seibu Shinjuku
Numabukuro
Nogata
❷
❸
Araiyakushi-M
NAKANO
❹

Kichijoji
Nishi-Ogikubo
JR Chuo
Ogikubo
Asagaya ❻
❺
Koenji
Nakano

Minami-asagaya
Shin-koenji
Higashi-koenji
Shin-naka

SUGINAMI
Nakanofujimicho
❽

MITAKA
❼
Honancho

Keio Inokashira
Nishi-Eifuku
Eifukucho
Hatagaya
❾
Meidai-Mae
Daitabashi
Yoyogi-ueha

Roka-koen
Chitose-karasuyama
Hachimanyama
Keio
Meidai-Mae
Daitabashi

Sengawa
❿
⓫
⓮
Gotokuji
Odakyu

CHOFU
Chitose-
Funabashi
Kyodo
⓬
Sangen-jaya
⓳
Odakyu
Soshigaya-Okura
⓭
⓰
SETAGAYA
⓴
Tokyu Denen-toshi

Seijogakuen-Mae
⓮
⓱ ⓲
㉑
Komazawa-
daigaku
⓯
⓰
Sakurashinmachi
㉒
Yoga
㉓ ㉔

KOMAE
㉕
Toritsudaigak
㉖
MEGUR

㉛
Futakotamagawa
Kaminoge
Tokyu Oimachi
Todoroki
Jiyugao
㉚ ㉙ ㉘
Oyamadai
Kuhonbutsu
㉗

Tamagawa

KAWASAKI

N

0   1   2 km

Setagaya / Suginami / Nakano

BRONZE MONUMENT TO GUNDAM

In tribute to RX-78

3-32-1 Kami-Igusa, Suginami-ku (東京都杉並区上井草 3-32-1)
Kami-Igusa station (上井草), Seibu-Shinjuku lin

Of course the massive statue of Gundam RX-78[1] in Odaiba is a great tourist attraction, but there's another one for purists and fans at Kami-Igusa. Erected in March 2008, the bronze monument dedicated to Gundam (standing 3 metres high) reigns over the southern exit of the station, above a small container for fans to throw in their coins as an offering.

The statue, entitled *Daichi kara* (大地から), a reference to *Gundam Rising*, the first episode of the series *Gundam daichi ni tatsu* – ガンダム大地に立つ – Mobile Suit Gundam), is simply raising its arm to the skies.

Even the station bell has a Gundam theme

The Seibu-Shinjuku line enters Suginami ward from the west and heads towards the little-used Kami-Igusa station, through the downmarket suburbs of Chuo with their modest residential neighbourhoods.

Kami-Igusa, however, has a certain reputation among fans of giant robots. The Sunrise animation studio, Gundam's creator, has its main offices at 2-44-10 Kami-Igusa (not open to the public) in a quiet building right in the centre of the shopping street south of the station.

Apart from Sunrise, several other studios have opened since the 1970s in the area around the station, which is now trying to cash in on this history as the sacred home of animation, to the point that even the train departure bell has been replaced by the Gundam theme tune.

The outline of the robot is everywhere, from flags in the street to shop blinds.

[1] *Giant robot from the cult science-fiction franchise Gundam.*

PHILOSOPHICAL BUILDINGS OF TETSUGAKUDO PARK

Completely devoted to philosophy

1-34-28 Matsugaoka, Nakano-ku (東京都中野区松が丘 1-34-28)
15 minutes from Araiyakushi-mae station (新井薬師前), Seibu-Shinjuku line
Open 8am–6pm April to September, 9am–5pm October to March; closed 29–31 December

From a genial and absurd idea of Inoue Enryo,[1] Meiji thinker and founder of Toyo University, Tetsugakudo-koen (哲学堂公園 – Philosophy Hall Park) opened in 1904 along the banks of the Myoshojigawa, a 15-minute walk from Numabukuro. Entirely devoted to philosophical theory in physical form, the park is a quirky place that makes you think.

Within an area of just over 5 hectares, the park has the humble goal of "embodying all philosophy" through a collection of buildings, statutes and objects dispersed around a pretty urban park, part of which dates from the early 20th century.

The main buildings are concentrated around the Jikugo mound (時空岡), symbolizing the "philosophical space-time", to use the official terminology.

The little Shiseido shrine (四聖堂 – Shrine of the Four Saints), in the heart of the park, is dedicated to Confucius, Socrates, Kant and Buddha. Not open to the public. Next door is the beautiful Rokukendai tower (六賢台 – Stand of the Six Scholars), given over to six Eastern philosophers: the Japanese Prince Shotoku and Sugawara no Michizane, the Chinese Zhuangzi and Zhu Xi, and the Indians Nagarjuna and Kapila Maharshi. The small Mujinzo storeroom (無尽蔵) holds objects collected during Inoue's voyages. The philosopher also built a library, the Zettaijo (絶対城). Farther along, a statue of Prince Shotoku stands inside the Uchukan (宇宙館 – Palace of the Universe), a wooden building erected to recall that philosophy aims to investigate the truth of the universe. The park is dotted with other sculptures and objects that are not always easy to interpret, even with the help of the noticeboards. To top this mysterious ensemble, the small Garden of Philosophy lies on the southern edge of the park. It contains statues by Nandor Wagner[2] installed in 2009 around three rings representing different thinkers and religious figures. The first ring includes statues of Jesus, Buddha, Lao Tzu, Abraham and Pharaoh Akhenaton. These statues are just above a huge overflow reservoir of the very capricious Myoshojigawa.

[1] 井上円了, *1858–1919.*
[2] *1922–1997. Hungarian artist and sculptor.*

ENTRANCE TO NAKANO PRISON ③

A rare example of a brick building from the early 20th century

3-37-3 Arai, Nakano-ku (東京都中野区新井 3-37-3)
10-minute walk from Numabukuro station (沼袋), Seibu-Shinjuku line
Usually closed to the public but easy to see inside the grounds

The Tokyo training centre for correctional facility staff is located just south of Heiwa no Mori Park. In the grounds you'll notice a very graceful solitary red-brick building that contrasts with the others. This is the former main entrance to Nakano prison (旧中野刑務所正門), the early 20th century successor to Toyotama, where political and other prisoners were incarcerated.

This entrance, the only relic of the penitentiary, dates from 1915, making it one of the city's few examples of a brick construction to have survived the 1923 earthquake. From the street you can see the back of the entrance, as if from inside the grounds.

Numerous writers and activists have passed through it, such as anarchist Osugi Sakae[1] in 1919, and Toda Josei[2] during the war. After the war, the facility was converted to a military prison by the Allied forces and GIs were kept there before being repatriated to the United States.

Handed back to the Japanese in 1957, it then became Nakano prison and an emphasis was placed on rehabilitation programmes.

Two prisoners did, however, escape in January 1961 after killing a guard, but they were caught the next day.

When the prison was built this was a very low-density area, but the extension of Tokyo caught up with it after the war. Under pressure from the increasing number of local residents, the prison finally closed in 1983.

> Heiwa no Mori Park was opened in 1985 on the site of the former prison. The park is beautifully landscaped, with a series of small ponds on the north side. There is a concrete replica of a Yayoi habitation, as archaeological excavations after the prison was demolished revealed several artefacts from that period. A modest but free exhibition hall, good for a quick visit, is devoted to the history of the district during the war and the bombings. In summer, a free mini-pool is open for small children.

NEARBY
Nakano Broadway residence ④
Little-known residence above a shopping mall

Best known for its speciality shops, Nakano Broadway was one of Tokyo's first mixed-use complexes, a Roppongi Hills of the 1960s. An obscure titbit for manga-loving visitors: on the upper floors is a residence where several celebrities of the genre have stayed.

The roof even has a swimming pool and private garden. After almost half a century, the complex is well maintained and nicely situated, justifying the fairly high rents for a building of this age.

But architectural tastes have changed, and Nakano Broadway is now a historical curiosity, like a luxury version of the post-war *danchi*.

Viewing the inside without an invitation from a resident or authorization from an estate agent is unfortunately out of the question, so you'll have to settle for the outside. A residents' entrance can be found in the mall, next to an information point.

---

[1] 大杉栄, 1885–1923. Essayist, anarchist, translator and activist.
[2] 戸田城聖, 1900–1958. Educator and publisher, one of the founders of the Soka Gakkai Buddhist movement.

PEARL CENTER STATUETTES

Venerable protectors of the arcade

Near 1-34 Minami-Asagaya, Suginami-ku (東京都杉並区阿佐ヶ谷南 1-34)
10-minute walk from Asagaya station (阿佐ヶ谷), JR Chuo line

In the middle of the Pearl Center shopping arcade (阿佐谷パールセンター), two very old and little-known statuettes, one of Jizo and the other of Shomen-Kongo, stand peacefully next to a florist, opposite a café, near 1-34 Minami-Asagaya.

As shown by the offerings of flowers, these two statuettes are always treated with great respect. They were installed in the late 17th century to watch over a pilgrims' route that now follows the line of the arcade. The Pearl Center was indeed on the old Gongen-michi route in the Kamakura era – it led to the temples of Enkoin (at Nukui, Nerima ward) to the north and Myoho-ji (at 3-Horinouchi) to the south.

The Tanabata Asagaya festival (阿佐ヶ谷七夕祭り), held in the Pearl Center arcade around 7 July, is a fairly recent tradition that dates from 1954. The arcade claims to be the oldest pedestrian-only shopping street in Tokyo Metropolis, having been closed to vehicles since 1952.

NEARBY

Asagaya Anime Street ⑥

New centre of anime culture

Part of the space under the Chuo line has been occupied since the end of March 2014 by Asagaya Anime Street (阿佐ヶ谷アニメストリート). Around a dozen shops, a mini-museum and even a (tiny) design school share the narrow but restored spaces, all more or less connected with anime, manga, video games and general Japanese pop culture. You can have a scan to create your own avatar or print a 3D statuette of yourself (obviously indispensable).

Stallholders tend to "cosplay" (costume or role play), and performance artists sometimes wander around. Simple snacks and coffee are on offer. Anime Street is still trying to find its feet and the enthusiastic atmosphere is appealing. Although the shops seem rather experimental and have yet to connect with their customers, all the ingredients are there to create a new hotspot of *anime* culture in the west of the city to compete with Nakano.

IRORI AT SUGINAMI HISTORICAL MUSEUM

A warming venue for cold winter days

1-20-8 Omiya, Suginami-ku (東京都杉並区大宮 1-20-8)
15-minute walk from Nagafukucho station (永福町), Keio Inokashira line
Open 9.30am–5pm, closed Mondays and third Wednesday of the month;
if those days are public holidays the museum is open, but closed the following
day; closed 28 December to 4 January
Admission: 100 yen
Irori fire lit on Saturdays, Sundays and public holidays

Suginami Historical Museum (杉並区立郷土博物館), near the Zenpukuji River, sets out the history of the district around some modest exhibits. Although the museum isn't very big, you can still spend a pleasant hour there in peace and quiet, discovering the past of one of the most residential districts of the capital.

The curiosity of this museum is an entire house dating from the late 18th century. Originally sited about 5 kilometres to the north-west, it was dismantled and transported here in 1973.

On Saturdays, Sundays and public holidays, the fire of the house *irori* is lit to welcome the few early-afternoon visitors, making it a perfect venue for cold winter days.

SACRED HALLS OF RISSHO KOSEI-KAI

Impressive architectural changes in modern Buddhism

2-11-1 Wada, Suginami-ku (東京都杉並区和田 2)
Fujimicho Nakano (中野富士見町) or Honancho (方南町) line; Tokyo metro
Marunouchi line

Emerging from the residential area of Suginami, south of Koenji at 2-11-1 Wada, is a monumental circular building encircled by eight turrets, with a 15-metre spike on the roof.

The Great Sacred Hall of Rissho Kosei-kai (立正佼成 会大聖堂), built in 1964 and renovated in 2006, is capped with a pagoda illuminated at night and protected by four guardian lions. The vast interior of the sacred hall is usually open to the public, although photos are not allowed.

Just behind the Sacred Hall is Horin-Kaku (法輪閣) and its exquisite modern Japanese garden, with another circular pagoda (一乗宝塔).

The Fumon Hall (普門館) at 2-6-1 Wada, a multipurpose venue almost as impressive as the Sacred Hall but with a less elaborate exterior, is another Rissho Kosei-kai centre. Until 2013 it housed the All Japan Band Competition, a national event for school bands, before an inspection reported serious reservations about the ceiling's resistance to earthquakes.

Rissho Kosei-kai

A Buddhist movement formed in the 1930s after a split with Reiyukai (霊友会), Rissho Kosei-kai is one of Japan's major Buddhist "new movements".

It claims over 3 million believers, although this figure has dropped significantly from a peak of 6.5 million in the 1990s. The movement strongly influences (or totally manages) a few blocks in the heart of Suginami. Kosei college and high school opposite Fumon Hall is also an offshoot of Rissho Kose-kai.

LA PORTA IZUMI NO MON AND MIND WAA RESIDENCES

Two dreamlike works by Von Jour Caux

1-4-8 and 2-27-27 Izumi, Suginami-ku (東京都杉並区和泉 1-4-8 / 2-27-27)
5 and 10 minutes from Daitabashi station (代田橋), Keio line
Accessible 24/7, living space closed to non-residents

Designed in the late 20th century by Von Jour Caux, two neighbouring apartment blocks known as La Porta Izumi no Mon (at 1-4-8 Izumi) and Mind Waa (at 2-27-27 Izumi) are examples of this architect's eccentric style.

As with his other works, there's not much restraint. Tile mosaics with mixed patterns and colours abound among all manner of decorative excrescences.

The façades of La Porta have some original sculptures, notably a large body with feminine curves surrounded by stained glass at the main entrance, while a winged Pegasus seems to be taking off from the roof. A statuette of a menacing-looking animal watches over the entrance to the residence, and the windows let a colourful play of light into the lobby. Access to the rest of the building is restricted to residents, but the outside is striking enough.

Mind Waa, a few blocks away, is a little less curvy and more angular. The façade is covered with multicoloured carved square decorations in relief. The few parts visible to non-residents are visually loaded. The ground floor is home to a convenience store, which you can of course enter, but the inside is completely bog-standard – a moment's rest before facing all the extravagances of the façades again.

For more on Von Jour Caux and his various works in Tokyo, see following double-page spread.

Von Jour Caux, the Japanese Gaudí

Dubbed the "heretic architect" and the "Japanese Gaudí" for his designs, some very uninhibited, Von Jour Caux (梵寿綱), real name Tanaka Toshiro (田中俊郎), was born in 1934 in Asakusa, Tokyo. After studying at Waseda University and the School of the Art Institute of Chicago, he began an unconventional architect's career

Building and completion date	Location
エステエスペランザ Est!!! Esperanza 1976	東京都港区西麻布2-17-14 2-7-14 Nishi-Azabu Minato-ku
秘羅禧：ルボア平喜 Hiraki: Le Bois Hiraki 1977	京都板橋区高島平1-76-14 1-76-14 Takashimadaira Itabashi-ku
斐醴祈：ルボア平喜南池袋 Hiraki: Le Bois Hiraki Minami Ikebukuro, 1979	東京都豊島区南池袋2-29-16 2-29-16 Minami-Ikebukuro Toshima-ku
Waseda El Dorado 1984	東京都新宿区早稲田鶴巻町517 517 Waseda Tsurumakicho Shinjuku-ku
Petit Etang 1987	東京都豊島区池袋3-51-5 3-51-5 Ikebukuro Toshima-ku
La Porta：和泉の門 La Porta Izumi no Mon 1989	東京都杉並区和泉1-4-8 1-4-8 Izumi Suginami-ku
Royal Vessel：輝く器 Royal Vessel Kagayaku utsuwa, 1990	東京都豊島区南池袋2-31-3 2-31-3 Minami-Ikebukuro Toshima-ku
舞都和亜 Mind Waa, 1992	東京都杉並区和泉2-27-27 2-27-27 Izumi Suginami-ku

before taking a pseudonym and in 1974 founding Von Jour Caux and his Art Complex (梵寿綱と仲), breaking with the norm.

Waseda El Dorado is probably his most complete work in Tokyo, but several other buildings are worth a visit for the touch of fantasy they bring to the city.

Description and characteristics

Commercial premises and offices, imposing stained-glass window on façade

---

Apartment block, decorative stained-glass entrance, façade with sculptures

---

Offices of alcohol wholesaler Hiraki:

besides the protective grilles and finely decorated façade, two black orbs seem to watch passers-by from corner of building

---

Apartment block

Apartment block (studios), impressive carved entrance

Apartment block, massive inlaid statue of a female body

Small commercial and office building

Small commercial and office building
da un convenience store

FORMER RESIDENCE OF TOKUTOMI ROKA

Sober and simple residence of a great writer

1-20 Kasuya, Setagaya-ku (東京都世田谷区粕谷 1-20)
15-minute walk from Roka-koen station (芦花公園), Keio line
Open 9am–4pm, closed 29 December to 3 January
Admission free

The last home of writer and philosopher Tokutomi Roka, in Roka-Koshunen (蘆花恒春園), was left to the city by his widow in the 1930s and the park and gardens were named in his honour.

The little house hidden among the trees was built in the early 20th century and faithfully restored in the 1980s.

Its sober and remarkably simple style reflects the country's rapid transformation and Westernization at the turn of the century.

There are three interconnected buildings a short distance apart. The main house (母屋 – *moya*), with a thatched roof, has Western toilets – a rarity at the time.

There's also an old-fashioned *goemonburo* (cast-iron bathtub heated from underneath with firewood).

The first annex, *Baikashooku* (梅花書屋 – Study with Plum Blossoms), dates from 1909 and is named after an example of horizontal calligraphy (still on display) by Samejima Hakkaku.[1]

The second annex, *Shusuishoin* (秋水書院 – Study of Shusui), dates

from 1911. Kotoku Shusui[2] was executed on the very day that the building was inaugurated.

Tokutomi, who had tried to seek clemency for what he considered a clear case of judicial error, dedicated the building to Kotoku (secretly at first). The tomb of the writer and his wife lies a short distance to the east of the house.

The park also has a free exhibition centre and memorial dedicated to Tokutomi, opened in the 1950s. Several of his personal effects can be seen, including a letter from Leo Tolstoy, whom he had visited in 1906.

Tokutomi Roka

Tokutomi Roka (original name, Tokutomi Kenjiro) was born in Kumamoto in 1868, as the Meiji era began. Between 1898 and 1899 he published *Hototogisu* (不如帰 – The Cuckoo, which appeared in English as *Namiko*), a melodramatic serial tale of parental interference in a young marriage, which was an overnight success. The following year, he moved to Kasuya, in what was still countryside and was to become his last home. In 1912 he published *Mimizu no tawagoto* (みみずのたはこと - *Gibberish of an Earthworm*), which reflects "peasant" life on his new country estate. He died in 1927, just after a reconciliation with his brother, the well-known journalist Tokutomi Soho,[3] whom he considered was drifting too far to the right politically.

[1] 鮫島白鶴, *1774–1859. Calligrapher of the Satsuma clan.*
[2] 幸徳秋水, *1871–1911. Journalist, anarchist, thinker of the Meiji era, convicted of high treason (probably wrongly) for taking part in an attempt to assassinate the emperor in 1910.*
[3] 徳富蘇峰, *1863–1957.*

SOSHIGAYA PARK'S TWO NOTORIOUS HOUSES

At the heart of the Setagaya murder mystery

3-22-19 Kami-Soshigaya, Setagaya-ku (東京都世田谷区上祖師谷 3-22-19)
20-minute walk from Senkawa station (仙川), Keio line, or 5 minutes from
Komadai-Grand Mae bus stop (駒大グランド前); lines 歳20, 歳21, 成02, 成
06 from Seijo-Gakuenmae station (成城学園前), Keio line
Accessible 24/7

Just over a kilometre south of the Keio railway line, after a longish walk through the residential area or a short bus ride, you reach the point where the Senkawa flows through the little park of Soshigaya (祖師谷公園).

Towards the centre of the park, along the riverside, two detached houses seem to stand alone in the landscape.

Curiously, they often have a police guard and a tarpaulin covers the area at the back to conceal it from children playing in the park.

The house nearest the river was the site of one of the hottest news stories in Japan and one of the last great criminal mysteries of the 20th century. On the night of 30 to 31 December 2000, an entire family of four was killed by an assailant who, judging by several clues (leftovers in the fridge, internet log, etc.), spent almost half a day at the crime scene, probably behaving "normally" without giving any signs of suspicious behaviour. The husband's mother, who lived in the house next door (the other guarded house), discovered the bodies on the morning of the 31st. Tens of thousands of police officers were involved in the investigation

to try and find the culprit. Judging by the scale of the resources employed, the strange behaviour of the murderer, and the emotion aroused at the last New Year of the century, the murder of the family at Setagaya has made a lasting impression.

These two houses weren't the only ones in the park at the time, but the neighbours preferred to move after the gruesome happenings at the site. Their houses were demolished and only these two remain. Both houses, from their slight elevation, take on a positively gloomy air as evening falls.

MANEKI-NEKO
AT GOTOKU-JI

⑫

Another possible source of Maneki-neko
in a charming temple to the west

2-24-7 Gotoku-ji, Setagaya-ku (東京都世田谷区豪徳寺 2-24-7)
Miyanosaka station (宮の坂), Setagaya line
Open 9am–4.30pm daily

Not far from Miyanosaka station, Gotoku-ji (豪徳) seems to be the source of *Maneki-neko*, in direct competition with the Imado shrine at Asakusa (see p. 264), which also claims parentage of the lucky cat, according to another legend.

It's here that Ii Naotaka,[1] the feudal lord (*daimyo*) of Hikone, while out with his falcons, is said to have sheltered from a storm in the temple where there was a cat, and to have befriended the temple priest while the rain fell. Following their meeting, the temple became the *bodaiji* (Buddhist "bodhi temple") of the Ii lords of Hikone.

Cat or not, the temple is a beautiful secluded site to the west of the city. The compound includes (besides the endless cat statuettes) a splendid-looking pagoda, even if not original.

Keen historians can also visit the graves of the Ii lords, who are buried behind this most charming of temples.

[1] 井伊直孝, 1590–1659. 2nd lord of Hikone, 25th lord of Ii and son of Ii Naomasa, one of Tokugawa Ieyasu's leading generals.

ULTRAMAN OF SOSHIGAYA-OKURA

Origin of the Tokusatsu

*1-8 Soshigaya-Okura, Setagaya-ku (*東京都世田谷区祖師谷大蔵1-8*)*
*In front of Soshigaya-Okura station (*代田橋*), Odakyu line*
Accessible 24/7

The real Ultraman weighs 35,000 tonnes and stands 40 metres tall (that's what it takes to effectively defend the Earth against alien attacks since his first TV appearance in 1966). So it's a very small Ultraman statue, almost human in size, that watches over the north exit of Soshigaya-Okura station.

In the tradition of many traders in unfrequented outlying districts, who borrow characters from popular culture to try and attract customers, those around Soshigaya-Okura clubbed together in 2005, and the following year, they set up this statue on the station concourse.

The former studios responsible for the original Ultraman, Tsuburaya Productions, were located in the area (they have since moved near Shibuya).

NEARBY
Other traces of Ultraman ⑭

The station statue isn't the only trace of Ultraman in the district. Going north up the shopping street for just over a kilometre, you'll find a flying Ultraman at 6-19 Soshigaya. There's also a statue of Ultraman Zoffy due west towards 3-21 Soshigaya, and one of Ultraman Jack to the south near 8-1 Kinuta. Soshigaya-Okura is well defended…

ROTATING BUDDHA OF OKURA

High-tech Buddha

5-12-3 Okura, Setagaya-ku (東京都世田谷区大蔵 5-12-3)
15 minutes from Seijogakuen-mae station (成城学園前), Odakyu line
Open 9am–6pm daily – statue rotates at around 9am and 5pm

Along the Senkawa at 5-12-3 Okura lie the precincts of Myohou-ji, a temple of the Nichiren Buddhist sect. At the end of the rows of graves, towards the river, you'll find a pet cemetery with the Great Buddha of Okura (おおくら大仏) standing next to it. This bronze statue, standing 8 metres high and weighing 8 tonnes, is an amazing but little-known high-tech Buddha, built in 1994 during the Buddhist celebrations of the autumn equinox (秋のお彼岸 – *o-higan*).

The benevolent Buddha, on its rotating base, changes direction every day. From 9am, he looks to the south, the cemetery, the faithful and the temple. By late afternoon, around 5pm, the statue rotates and will cast his gaze towards Setagaya-dori, protecting the traffic and children coming home from school. The statue's pivot mechanism, which is quite slow, is surprisingly quiet.

If the temple is closed, you don't need to go inside the enclosure to see the statue – it's visible from the river and Okura *danchi*.

NEARBY

Godzilla statue at the entrance to Toho Studios ⑯

Facing the Seven Samurai

South of the Odakyu line, both banks of the Senkawa are occupied by the gigantic installations of Toho Studios (東宝スタジオ) at 1-4-1 Seijo. They are among the biggest in the country, and gave Godzilla and the Kurosawa masterpieces to movie fans.

The studios, which were almost completely refurbished in the 2000s, are unfortunately not open to the public.

You'll have to console yourself with a very effective Godzilla statue at the main entrance in front of a photographic mural of the Seven Samurai. The monster's tail seems to have become violently embedded in a wall.

Just in front of the statue, another façade of the studio entrance was decorated in May 2014 with a huge portrait of Godzilla.

Although you can't access the studios, the promenade along the banks, covered with cherry trees and illuminated at night in the flowering season, is accessible all year round.

FOOD AND AGRICULTURE MUSEUM

Stuffed chickens in their hundreds

2-4-28 Kami-Yoga, Setagaya-ku (東京都世田谷区上用賀 2-4-28)
20-minute walk from Yoga station (用賀), Tokyu Den-en-Toshi line; Nodaimae
bus stop (農大前); Tokyu 園02 or Tokyu 用01 lines from Yoga station
Open 10am–5pm April to November, 10am–4.30pm December to March,
every day except Monday – if a public holiday falls on a Monday the museum
is open, but closed the following day; closed fourth Tuesday of the month;
extended closure during August and year-end celebrations
Admission free

As its name suggests, the Food and Agriculture Museum (食と農博物館), which is part of the Setagaya campus of Tokyo University of Agriculture, is dedicated to agricultural technologies and the history of food.

Particular noteworthy are the hundreds of specimens of stuffed chickens of different varieties displayed upstairs. In addition to domesticated varieties from Japan and elsewhere, you can also discover the wild ancestors of the common chicken. Besides the chickens, the museum has a collection of sake bottles to rival the best-stocked bars. At the entrance there are sometimes a few live chickens cackling in cages. This unique exhibition reminds stressed city dwellers (who rarely get to see live chickens in one piece) how important this bird is in their diet.

The entrance to this modern cubic building seems to be protected by a curious and imposing statue of a rooster. Inside is a display of vintage farm tools from around the country (the museum claims to have about 3,600 pieces).

NEARBY
Biorium ⑱
Tropical experiments
Right next to the museum, a tropical greenhouse known as the Biorium (バイオリウム) – offshoot of the university's Agricultural Research Institute – also arranges tours. The Biorium is directly accessible via the museum.

WAYMARKER AT OYAMA-DORI

Ancient pilgrimage route

2-13 Sangenjaya, Setagaya-ku (東京都世田谷区三軒茶屋 2-13)
Sangenjaya station (三軒茶屋), Tokyu Toyoko line; Tokyu Setagaya tram
Accessible 24/7

J ust beside the Setagaya-dori exit of Sangenjaya station, you'll notice an old waymarker for a pilgrims' route, rather forlornly standing in this modern urban environment dominated by expressways.

The pilgrimage, which blended Buddhism and popular mystical beliefs relating to Mount Oyama (where it led) in Kanagawa prefecture, was very popular in the early 19th century.

First installed in 1749 and restored in the early 19th century, the waymarker was moved during construction work for the 1964 Olympics,

then relocated here in 1983, very close to its historic site.

The name of the neighbourhood (三軒茶屋 – Three Tearooms) comes from the three tearooms frequented by pilgrims and located beside the waymarker: Kadoya (角屋), Tanakaya (田中屋) and Ishibashiro (石橋楼). All of them are now gone:

Kadoya closed in the Meiji era, Tanakaya burned down, and Ishibashiro was evacuated in 1945.

Sangenjaya triangle

The tiny area south of Sangenjaya station – and in particular, the tip of the triangle formed by the junction of two streets, Setagaya-dori and Tamagawa-dori, generally corresponding to 2-13 Sangenjaya – is dotted with small bars and *izakaya* (gastropubs) around some gloomy alleys. These establishments are frequented by a certain group of Tokyo youth at the forefront of fashion, in a setting worthy of the most retro corners of the north-east of the city. This triangle, with its post-war mood, is in marked contrast to its surroundings, which have been devastated by urban redevelopment. It's one of those remote but chic places where you must have a drink at least once, and where you have to know the best places in order to qualify as a real Tokyoite. In some ways, one of the hotspots in the life of the trendy youth of Tokyo.

SETAGAYA MUSEUM OF HISTORY ⑳

First local history museum in Metropolitan Tokyo

1-29-18 Setagaya, Setagaya-ku (東京都世田谷区世田谷 1-29-18)
3-minute walk from Kamimachi station (上町), Tokyu Setagaya tram
Open 9am–5pm every day except Monday – if a public holiday falls on
a Monday the museum is open, but closed the following day; open for Day
of Culture (3 November) and Boro-Ichi flea market

All the local museums in Tokyo's wards are interesting in their own way, but Setagaya Museum of History (世田谷区立郷土資料館) is definitely ahead of the game.

This neighbourhood museum, covering about 30,000 years of the history of the city's most populous (but far from most touristic) ward, opened in 1964.

This is actually the oldest museum of its kind in Tokyo. Although there's some fine ancient pots, paintings and calligraphy and well-made dioramas, it's not a national museum and the rare visitors probably won't see anything remarkable, but the short tour is free and friendly.

To add to its charm, the elegant building housing the museum collection is the work of Maekawa Kunio,[1] making it a monument in itself.

Best of all, the museum is on the same site as the well-preserved residence of the governor of Setagaya in the Edo period (代官 – *Daikan*), dating from the 18th century.

The residence, classed as an Important Cultural Property, is the only one of its kind to have survived in Tokyo Metropolis.

The *Boro-Ichi* flea market (ボロ市) is held on the 15th and 16th of the months of December and January, in the street in front of the governor's residence. The event, which goes back 400 years, has become one of the high points of street life in Setagaya, attracting crowds from far and wide.

---

[1] 前川国男, 1905–1986. A leading figure of 20th century Japanese architecture.

TOWERS OF KOMAZAWA WATER SUPPLY STATION

A spectacular and little-known relic of the Taisho era

2-41-5 Tsurumaki, Setagaya-ku (東京都世田谷区弦巻 2-41-5)
10-minute walk from Sakurashinmachi station (桜新町),
Tokyu Den-en-Toshi line
Exterior visible from the street
Tours of the interior offered once a year, usually 1 October for Tomin no hi
(都民の日), Tokyo residents' day
See Koma-Q site (http://setagaya.kir.jp/koma-q/) for more information

The twin towers of the Komazawa Water Supply Station (駒沢給水所), among the houses around Sakurashinmachi, are a spectacular but little-known relic of the Taisho era (1912–1926). The towers were completed in 1924, just as the city's modern water distribution network was getting under way.

The water came from the Tama River, to be stored and redistribut-

ed around the expanding residential areas towards the city of Shibuya, which was absorbed in Tokyo in 1932 as part of Shibuya ward.

The water towers survived the Great Kanto Earthquake of 1923, during the construction work (one of the towers was already finished), as well as World War II, without extensive damage.

A planned third tower was never built.

The station hasn't been used as a distribution centre since the late 20th century, and is now simply a monument to Tokyo's water supply. It has been classed as local landscape heritage by Setagaya ward and as a heritage site by the Japanese Society of Civil Engineers.

Unfortunately, the premises are only open to the public once a year, during visits organized by the Komazawa Water Tower Preservation Society, Koma-Q (link above).

However, the two magnificent 30-metre water towers, built on an elevated spot to take advantage of gravity, can easily be seen from the street. Like a medieval European fortress, they dominate the low houses in these rarely visited depths of Setagaya.

STATUES OF *SAZAE* AND HER FAMILY AT SAKURASHINMACHI

Sazae at home

1-30-6 Sakurashinmachi, Setagaya-ku (東京都世田谷区桜新町 1-30-6)
Exit of Sakurashinmachi station (桜新町), Tokyu Den-en-Toshi line
Accessible 24/7

Before visiting the Hasegawa Machiko[1] Art Museum, named after the creator of the comic strip *Sazae-san*, have a look at the statues of manga characters at each exit of Sakurashinmachi station: Tara and Sazae at the south exit, Katsuo and Wakame at the north exit, the whole family (Sazae, Masuo, Tara, Namihei, Fune, Katsuo and Wakame) at the west exit. A solitary statue of Sazae herself also watches over the Sazae-san *koban* at 1-30-14 Sakurashinmachi. The whole family gathers one last time in the park just behind the museum.

NEARBY

Hasegawa Machiko Art Museum ㉓
Sazae's origins

Hasegawa Machiko Art Museum, opened in 1985, is at the end of the aptly named Sazae-san-dori, at 1-30-6 Sakurashinmachi. The place is more a general arts museum, which isn't really much to do with Sazae, even though there's a diorama on the first floor of the home of the Fuguta[2] and Isono families.

The museum, in a small red-brick two-storey building open every day except Monday, brings together part of the personal collections of Machiko and her sister Mariko. The displays (ranging from pottery to paintings) are regularly changed.

Sazae-san e Sakurashinmachi

With over 7,000 short stories broadcast over almost 2,300 episodes, Sazae is far ahead of the *Simpsons* in *Guinness World Records*. Sakurashinmachi, where Sazae and her family live, perhaps had a semi-suburban air in the post-war period, when Hasegawa Machiko was drawing her manga cartoons as four-frame strips reflecting a life where nothing really serious could happen, but the setting of remote, quiet suburbs no longer exists. Nowadays Sakurashinmachi is overlooked by middle-class homes, the small shops effaced by a huge shopping mall, and the train runs underground. Sazae and family hold the area around Sakurashinmachi station in their frail hands, making you wonder if the neighbourhood rents will also go under should the TV programme, broadcast every Sunday night since 1969, ever be dropped.

---

[1] 長谷川町子, 1920–1992.
[2] フグ田, *Sazae's family name. Born Isono Sazae, she lives in a multigenerational household with her husband Masuo, their son Tarao (Tara-chan), her parents Namihei and Fune Isono, her younger brother Katsuo and sister Wakame.*

THE *SANDO* AT HISATOMI-INARI SHRINE

Original pilgrims' road in the heart of the city

2-17-1 Shinmachi, Setagaya-ku (東京都世田谷区新町 2-17-1)
10-minute walk from Sakurashinmachi station (桜 新 町),
Tokyu Den-en-Toshi line

The remarkable 250-metre sando (path from *torii* to shrine), leading to Hisatomi-Inari shrine (久富稲荷神社), is surmounted by several *torii*. It gives you an insight into residential Setagaya via a short walk where Shinto blends into the urban fabric – quite a curiosity in Tokyo.

The entrance to what was originally a pilgrims' road lies approximately 500 metres east of Sakurashinmachi along Route 427. Most of the time the road is practically deserted except for local residents, but it comes alive twice a year (usually in May and November) for a small second-hand market.

Those who have walked through the 10,000 *toriis* on the way to Fushiimi-Inari Taisha[1] at Kyoto will find a simplified Tokyo version here.

Inside the main shrine, a small annex is dedicated to the owl. The story goes that in the Showa era a very elusive owl sometimes hooted at night. According to tradition, anyone who had the chance to see (or hear, depending on the version) the owl would have their wishes granted. Nocturnal visitors be warned.

Commemorating this story, the shrine's ema are decorated with sketches of an owl, and the local markets are known as *Fukuro Matsuri* (フクロウ祭り – Owl Festival).

The history of Hisatomi-Inari shrine, mentioned as protector of a nearby village of the Edo era, is still fairly vague. It was rebuilt and restored in the 20th century by local worshippers.

[1] *Thought to be scarcely more than 3,000...*

GALLERY OF THE MEMORIAL AT KOMAZAWA OLYMPIC PARK

Below the secondary site of the 1964 Games

1-1 Komazawa-koen, Setagaya-ku (東京都世田谷区駒沢公園 1-1)
15 minutes from Komazawa-Daigaku (駒澤大学), Tokyu Den-en-Toshi line
Open 9.30am–5pm every day except first and third Mondays of the month –
if a public holiday falls on a Monday the gallery is open, but closed the
following day; closed 31 December to 2 January
Admission free

In the basement of the gymnasium of Komazawa Olympic Park, an uncrowded gallery commemorates the Summer Olympics of 1964. In addition to a series of contemporary photographs and posters, there's a collection of uniforms and tracksuits that show just how quickly fashions change.

The Olympic torch and some medals are also on display, and highlights from the Games can be viewed on the screens.

The exhibition is quite low-key, but the tour is free and lets you slip back easily into some of the euphoria of Japan's economic miracle.

Komazawa Olympic Park and the 1940 Games

Most of the events of the 1964 Olympic Games were held near Shinanomachi and Sendagaya. Komazawa Olympic Park (駒沢 オリンピック公園), a little farther from the centre, hosted side events including volleyball or football on the site of a former golf course. The park failed in its bid to become the main site of the 1940 Olympic Games. Tokyo had indeed been chosen in 1932 for the 1940 Summer Games, cancelled because of the second Sino-Japanese War. After the war, the main stadium for the Toei Flyers baseball team (now the Hokkaido Nippon-Ham Fighters) was built before the site was converted from 1962 to host this (small) part of the 1964 Olympics, adding various arenas and gymnasia.

In the large park, you can now immerse yourself in the beautiful architectural surroundings of the 1960s, as concrete and angular as you could wish. The central square is dominated by a 50-metre memorial tower resembling a large but elegant concrete skewer. The Olympic flame burned in a chalice set in the middle of the body of water east of the tower.

NEARBY

Edan Mall Fukasawa ㉖

A piece of Shitamachi to the south-west

In a more than affluent residential area (the surrounding districts are among the richest outside Yamanote) towards 3 Fukasawa, the mysterious Edan Mall Fukasawa (エーダンモール深沢) officially bears the shopping arcade's name of Higashi Fukasawa (東深沢商店街). This remarkable cluster of narrow shops, small bars and slightly crumbling *izakayas* would absolutely not work in the city's most remote north-east corners.

The origin of "Edan"

This tiny piece of Shitamachi originates in a social housing complex (都 営団地 – *Toei-danchi*) built to rehouse the victims of the great bombardment of Tokyo. Local shops were gradually established in the complex. "ToEi DANchi" has been shortened to "Eidan", which became "Edan", and this very narrow chequered neighbourhood that clashes so much with the surrounding streets.

KUHONBUTSU STATION

Station too short for the trains

7 Okuzawa Setagaya (東京都世田谷区奥沢世田谷 7)
Kuhonbutsu station (九品仏), Tokyu Oimachi line

The small station of Kuhonbutsu (九品仏駅), near Jiyugaoka, is a curiosity well worth a visit. The platform is too short to take the trains with five carriages that stop there.

When a train arrives, the doors of the carriage beyond the platform don't open, so you have to walk through the train to get off. Since the extension of the Togoshi-Koen station platform on the Tokyu Oimachi line in February 2013, Kuhonbutsu is Tokyo's only remaining example of a platform that's too short.

Incidentally, some doors don't open on the Isezaki line at Asakusa, not because of the length of the platform but because it's considered dangerous towards the ends.

The western end of this platform is intersected by a level crossing, so can't be extended without major work.

TODOROKI GORGE (28)

A canyon in the city

1-22 Todoroki, Setagaya-ku (東京都世田谷区等々力 1-22)
2-minute walk from Todoroki station (等々力), Tokyu Oimachi line
Accessible 24/7

This natural gorge – eroded over thousands of years on the slopes of Musashino plateau by the Yazawa before it flows into the Tamaga-wa – is one of Tokyo's most remarkable parks.

The 10-metre gorge of Todoroki Valley Park (等々力渓谷公園) literally cuts the city in two.

Although this isn't Setagaya's version of the Grand Canyon, there's something almost mystical about strolling in your city shoes through a gorge over a kilometre long, deep enough to shut out the rumble of traffic and hide the concrete and glass of surrounding buildings.

The gorge has several interesting features, from Buddhist and Shinto sites to a (small) waterfall and even a kofun tomb with its entrance protected by a glass wall, all surrounded by lush greenery and birdsong. Change of scene guaranteed.

TUMULI ON MUSASHINO'S HILLSIDES

Ancestral graves in the city centre

2-12 Kaminoge, Setagaya-ku (東京都世田谷区上野毛 2-12) for Kaminoge-Inarizuka, 1-25 Noge Setagaya-ku (東京都世田谷区野毛 1-25) for Noge-Otsuka
8- to 10-minute walk from Kaminoge station (上野毛), Tokyu Oimachi line
Kaminoge-Inarizuka can be seen behind a barrier; Noge-Otsuka is accessible

At 2-12 Kaminoge, a strange little round green hill behind a barrier may well interest curious visitors.

Far from being a natural hill, it's the site of a keyhole tomb (前方後円墳) over fifteen centuries old – Kaminoge-Inarizuka tumulus (上野毛稲荷塚古墳).

Following excavations in 1995 and 2009, several artefacts such as necklaces were found, dating the mound to the end of the 4th century – one of the oldest in the area.

Some 500 metres away, in Tamagawanogemachi Park between the baseball pitch and the tennis courts and this time resembling a circular

pyramid, is the much more imposing No-ge-Otsuka tumulus (野毛大塚古墳), which was probably the tomb of a high-ranking warlord of the mid-5th century. Excavations in the late 19th century revealed thousands of objects.

The top of the mound, which stands 10 metres high, is accessible and you can see plans of the excavations.

Other burial mounds in the area

These two tumuli are not the only ones in this urban area: there are actually around fifty ancestral graves of various sizes along the banks of the Tamagawa between Tamagawa-en and Futako-Tamagawa stations.

One example is the tomb at Todoroki gorge (see p. 117). Detailed maps indicating all these little hills, some more obvious than others, are available locally: try the Ota Local History Museum at 5-11-13 Minami-Magome.

NEARBY ㉚

Kimura Budoen ("grape garden") and chicken run

Kimura Budoen (木村ぶどう園, 2-20-16 Noge), with its ancient tombs, is a subtle cross between an outdoor chicken run (the cackling of the chickens barely disturbs the peace), a vineyard and a strawberry patch. Anyone can come and pick grapes or strawberries here, depending on the season. Raccoon raids sometimes affect egg sales...

Steep slopes of Den-en-Chofu

A little farther east, the west side of the fan-shaped Den-en-Chofu neighbourhood is a reminder of why it was originally called Tamagawa heights. Circumnavigating the edge of Musashino plateau, the narrow streets tumble down from the heights to the Tama River over a series of vertiginous slopes that are often steeper than 20 degrees.

For example, near 5-5-18 Den-en-Chofu is the start of Umazaka (馬坂 – literally "Slope of the Horses"), where horses painfully ascended a 22-degree slope in the Taisho era. Between 5-26 and 5-27 Den-en-Chofu is Kyuzaka (急坂 – literally "Steep Hill"), a name that suits it perfectly. In the south-west corner of Tamagawa water treatment plant, between 5-13 Den-en-Chofu and 5-18 Den-en-Chofu, a nameless slope even reaches 26 degrees. 1 Oyamadai, west of 5 Den-en-Chofu, also has some really challenging terrain.

UNDERNEATH TAMAGAWA-DAISHI ㉛
TEMPLE

Make your pilgrimage in the dark

4-13-3 Seta, Setagaya-ku (東京都世田谷区瀬田 4-13-3)
10-minute walk from Futako-Tamagawa station (二子玉川),
Tokyu Den-en-Toshi or Oimachi lines
Open 9am–5pm

A few minutes from the family atmosphere of Futako-Tamagawa, Tamagawa-Daishi (玉川大師) is an extremely original and little-known temple in the south-west of the city, dating from 1925. Although it looks rather nondescript from the outside, its surprising secret lies underground. A subterranean gallery was opened in 1934 at a depth of 5 metres to allow Tokyo residents who couldn't visit the actual sites to make the pilgrimage to eighty-eight Shikoku temples and thirty-three Saigoku Kannon temples.

The gallery, which has about 300 statues, was used as a shelter during the war. The statues include a reclining Buddha, the largest in the metropolis. After descending the steps reached via the hondo (a small donation is strongly encouraged), the journey begins in complete darkness – touch and hearing are your only guides along generally smooth walls, probably a trying experience for anyone who's claustrophobic.

After a short walk that seems absolutely endless, you'll see a row of Buddha statues in a very dimly lit space.

It is then appropriate to pray to the Buddha corresponding to your age,[1] before exiting, spiritually (and literally) more enlightened. Taking photos is strictly prohibited in the gallery, and cameras have to be handed in before descending the steps.

[1] *Calculated in the traditional way (数え年), age at birth is 1, then another year is added for each new year.*

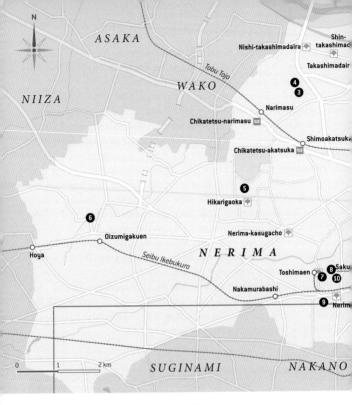

Nerima / Itabashi / Kita

TAKASHIMADAIRA ANTI-SUICIDE BARRIER

The dark past of a vast residential complex

2- and 3- Takashimadaira, Nerima-ku (東京都練馬区高島平 2-3)
Takashimadaira (高島平) or Shin-Takashimadaira (新高島平) stations,
Toei subway Mita line
Accessible 24/7

In the communal areas above the second floor of the gigantic Takashimadaira *danchi* (高島平団地), you'll see a metal barrier with rather artistic curved motifs.

These grilles, installed in 1981, aren't just for decoration. More prosaically, they're there to cut the number of suicides, as the height of the building has already tempted a number of people to hurl themselves into the void. The history of Takashimadaira (高島平 – *Plains of Takashima*, named after Takashima Shuhan,[1] who was the first to fire a Japanese-made cannon here in 1841) merges with that of the *danchi*, the mother of all the city's ageing mega-*danchi* built during the economic miracle. The housing complex, opened in 1972 shortly after the Mita subway line, is home to about 17,000 people, down from 30,000 at its peak in the late 1980s. Takashimadaira got off to a bad start: in 1972, five new residents took advantage of the fourteen-storey buildings to commit suicide.

On 13 April 1977, a father in despair at the disappearance of his wife and two children jumped, earning the *danchi* the "suicide mecca" nickname that it could well have done without. At the time, about one person a month was choosing to end their life here and the numbers grew as the tall buildings attract would-be suicides from all over Japan – over 80 per cent are not local.

In 1978 access to the roof was closed, and in 1981, the barrier was finally installed, dramatically reducing the number of deaths.

---

[1] 高島秋帆, *1798–1866. Military engineer and gunner in the late Edo period.*

YAKUSHI NO IZUMI GARDEN ②

Site of an old spring along the Nakasendo

3-7-20 Azusawa, Itabashi-ku (東京都板橋区小豆沢 *3-7-20*)
5-minute walk from Shimura-Sakaue station (志村坂上)*, Toei subway*
Mita line
Open daily 9am–4.30pm
Admission free

The welcoming Yakushi no Izumi garden (薬師の泉庭園), reached through a very low door (you'll have to stoop), directly on National Route 18, is actually a very successful copy dating from 1989.

Its very small scale means you can visit (or rather, walk through) the garden in 10 minutes at most, but this free tour is a pleasant break from the rumble of traffic on Route 18, which follows the old Nakasendo travellers' route to Kyoto from Edo via the centre of the country.

Even if the present garden is recent, its history goes back a long way. It was originally the site of Daizen-ji, a temple founded in the late 15th century and since absorbed by the neighbouring Sosen-ji.

Daizen-ji was built around a spring that has refreshed many a Nakasendo traveller. The 8th shogun, Tokugawa Yoshimune,[1] praised this water while he cooled off during a hunting party.

The venerated effigy (本尊 – *honzon*) of Daizen-ji was a Buddhist statuette of Bhaishajyaguru, the Buddha-healer (如来薬師 – *Nyorai Yakushi*), said to be the work of Prince Shotoku[2] in person. This Buddha, following the words of Yoshimune, was called the Buddha of the Source – hence the name of the garden (薬師の泉庭園, *Yakushi no Izumi Teien* – Garden of the Source of the Buddha-healer).

The source had already been depicted in the *Edo meisho zue* (江戸名所図 – Guide to Famous Places of Edo) in an engraving reproduced in the garden.

Times have changed, however: pilgrims no longer walk the Nakasendo, the garden is practically deserted, the spring is no more and to cool down you'll have to rely on automatic drinks dispensers.

---

[1] 徳川吉宗, *1684-1751.*
[2] 聖徳太子, *572–622, politician and regent when Buddhism arrived in Japan, alleged initiator of one of the country's first constitutions.*

GREAT BUDDHA OF TOKYO

Monumental yet little-known temple statue

5-28-3 Akatsuka, Itabashi-ku (東京都板橋区赤塚 5-28-3)
20-minute walk from Takashimadaira station (高島平), Tokyo metro Mita
line, or 20 minutes from Shimoakatsuka (下赤塚) or Narimasu (成増)
stations, Tobu-Tojo line
Open 10am–4pm daily

North-east of Narimasu, in the heart of Akatsuka neighbourhood, Joren-ji houses the Great Buddha of Tokyo (東京大仏), the third-largest bronze Buddha in Japan after those of Nara and Kamakura. The statue – oddly enough, only rarely mentioned in traditional guidebooks – was added as an offering after the temple was moved and rebuilt, to give thanks for the progress of the work.

The statue, a little over 12 metres in height, was erected in 1977. It's not as colossal as the above-mentioned Buddhas but still elegant and striking enough for its absence from city publicity to be surprising.

The distance from the nearest subway stations partly explains the tranquillity of the site, while the absence of noisy groups of students and crowds of foreign tourists fascinated by the deer at Nara's Todai-ji (Great Eastern Temple) only adds to its charm.

Founded between 1394 and 1427, Joren-ji was an important Edo temple. Until 1973, it stood at 62 Nakajuku, almost 7 kilometres southeast as the crow flies from its present site, next to Itabashi town hall and more importantly near the Nakasendo travellers' route and the Itabashi *shukuba* (post station or rest stop, see p. 154). It had to be moved following the construction of the urban expressway and widening of National Route 17, which encroached heavily on its grounds.

NEARBY
Commemorating Akatsuka castle   ④
Site of a lost castle

Joren-ji was rebuilt over part of the outer fortifications of Akatsuka castle, which belonged to the Chiba clan, allies of the Go-Hojo. Almost nothing remains of this castle, destroyed in the 16th century after the defeat of the Go-Hojo at the hands of Hideyoshi,[1] except a commemorative stone and noticeboard in Akatsuka-Tameike Park, explaining where the keep once stood. The castle occupied much of what is now 5-Akatsuka. Far from its grand past, Akatsuka has become a quiet residential neighbourhood consisting mainly of private houses and small apartments.

---

[1] 豊臣秀吉. *Toyotomi Hideyoshi, 1537-1598, one of the three feudal lords who unified the country in the 16th century.*

HIKARIGAOKA *DANCHI*

Tokyo's most impressive lineup of tower blocks

Hikarigaoka, Nerima-ku (東京都練馬区光が丘)
Hikarigaoka station (光が丘), Toei subway Oedo line

The massive residential community of Hikarigaoka Parktown (光が丘パークタウン), often referred to as *Hikarigaoka danchi*, is the largest in the city with 12,000 households and a population of over 35,000 over 186 hectares.

This is the equivalent of an average town, with fifteen schools and colleges, a hospital, a police station, supermarkets and small traders, all overlooking one of the largest parks in the city, an ideal vision of planned urban community life.

More than thirty years after opening, Hikarigaoka has kept an impressive, almost Soviet-style allure and is well worth a visit. It consists of a series of massive tall buildings, geometric and rather forbidding, around the perimeter.

The gigantic bike parking and waste disposal space of each residence is dominated by the lofty towers.

The initial oppressive impression is soon tempered by the friendliness of the residents, who are younger than the national average, a notable exception in these mega-*danchi*. Groups of children pedal recklessly among the pedestrians and wailing toddlers overflow in *Fureai no Michi*, the nickname of the central promenade. Ginkgos are planted along this agreeable route, which is maintained by the park it leads to. The IMA

shopping centre near the station at the end of Fureai no Michi is the biggest in Nerima.

The subway station, heart of the community and gateway to the rest of the city, opened in 1991. The Oedo line only went as far as Nerima at the time and there was no direct service to Shinjuku until late 1997. Hikarigaoka had to survive for a number of years with difficult access to the city centre, clearly forming a strong community.

Although the buildings have aged, everything is very well maintained.

Rice fields in the city

The *danchi* has three large seasonal parks (*Haru no Kaze*, 春の風公園 – Spring Wind Park; *Natsu no Kumo*, 夏の雲公園 – Summer Clouds Park; and *Aki no Hi*, 秋の陽公園 – Autumn Sun Park) that attempt to reproduce the original flora of Musashino plateau, breaking the uniformity of the rows of tower blocks.

Some rice is harvested in Autumn Sun Park. The fields are used by schools to grow rice that the children harvest (about 100 kilos each year).

Grant Heights or Grand Heights?

Hikarigaoka Parktown occupies the site of the Narimasu Air Force base (成増陸軍飛行所), built in 1943 to protect the city, whose relative vulnerability had been exposed by the Doolittle raid of 1942. The Nakajima Ki-44 fighter planes, replaced in 1945 by fifty formidable Ki-84 Hayates, were stationed there to defend the city from the increasingly frequent B-29 bomber raids. At the end of the war, the base was taken over by the Allies and razed to the ground, to be replaced by a housing estate of 1,200 units for families of US soldiers during the Occupation. The *34th Air Base Housing Area*, aka Grant Heights, opened in 1948. At the time, not many of the neighbours were familiar with the general and US president who gave his name to the base and this little bit of America was called "Grand" Heights. Given its size, "Grand" suits it perfectly.

In September 1973, Grant Heights was returned to the Japanese authorities. Plans were drawn up to build the monumental residential complex in 1977 and work began on the park to the north the same year. Construction of the housing began in 1981 and the first residents arrived in March 1983, days before the opening of Tokyo Disneyland.

KOIZUMI CATTLE

Downtown dairy farm

2-1-24 Oizumigakuencho, Nerima-ku (東京都練馬区大泉学園町 2-1-24)
15-minute walk from Oizumigakuen station (大泉学園), Seibu-Ikebukuro line
Ice-cream stall open 10am–5pm most days; cattle pens can be visited 24/7

Nerima, one of Tokyo's twenty-three "special wards" (*ku*), is interspersed with patches of farmland, clearly visible just off the main roads to the west.

Although the number of holdings is rapidly falling with urbanization, in 2009 there were still around 500 of them.

It's a 15-minute walk north from Oizumigakuen station to the last dairy herd in the area – Koizumi farm (小泉牧場), with its forty head of Holstein dairy cows.

A little stall on the street opposite the cattle pens sells artisan ice cream made with the farm's own milk, so you can appreciate on the spot the joys of city agriculture.

The site is easily detectable from a distance by the all-pervasive whiff of manure in what is otherwise a very urban landscape.

Farm visits are organized from time to time by local nurseries and elementary schools, so children can experience the joys of nature by feeding the animals.

You can sit down at a small table outside, right next to the pens, to peacefully enjoy an ice cream flavoured with chocolate, green tea or salt, close to the cattle and almost in the shadow of the farmhouse next door. This is of course the main point of the visit.

The local speciality is cabbage: Nerima ward is responsible for 40 per cent of the entire cabbage production of Tokyo Metropolis, including the rural towns and villages administered by the Metropolitan Government.

Nishi-Oizumicho: Tokyo's only administrative exclave

A 20-minute walk from Koizumi farm, around 100 metres north-west of the border between Nerima and Saitama, Nishi-Oizumicho (西大泉町) is a quirky little group of seven houses, the only administrative exclave in Tokyo's twenty-three wards.

One of the houses in the street is officially in the town of Niiza in Saitama prefecture, whereas its neighbour is in Tokyo's Nerima ward. Without going to the length of checking out people's addresses, you can see evidence of this administrative curiosity in a few details. Have a look at the manhole covers – some are the same design as in Tokyo. There's also a fire extinguisher in the Nerima colours. The electricity, telephone and water supplies are the responsibility of both Niiza and Saitama.

Back in Tokyo, the neighbourhood plan of the park at 2-23-1 Nishi-Oizumi clearly indicates the boundaries.

Neither Niiza nor Nerima seems to have any information on how this exclave came about, as nobody lived there until the 1970s.

Officially, Nerima would like to see it integrated with Niiza, but the (few) residents of Nishi-Oizumicho don't all agree: for the moment there is still an "island" of Tokyo in Saitama prefecture.

The station at Oizumigakuen (大泉学園 – Oizumi academic hub) is the nearest to Nishi-Oizumicho within a Tokyo ward.[1] Despite the name, it doesn't serve a university campus or research facility but the remote residential suburb of Ikebukuro, which developed in the 1920s after the Great Kanto Earthquake but failed to attract the higher educational institutes that would justify its name. There are of course some high schools, colleges and elementary schools, but no one would presume to call this very residential area a student heaven.

[1] *Another administrative curiosity ... Hoya station (保谷) is nearer Nishi-Oizumicho, but only a tiny section of the platform is in Nerima ward.*

SOBA-KUI JIZO OF KUHON'IN

Noodle-eating Jizo

4-25-1 Nerima, Nerima-ku (東京都練馬区練馬 4-25-1)
5-minute walk from Toshima-en station (豊 島 園), Toei subway Oedo
or Seibu Toshima lines

In Kuhon'in (九品院), one of the eleven temples of Tajima-san, you'll notice the curious *Soba-kui Jizo* (蕎麦喰地蔵 – Soba-Eating Jizo) to which offerings of soba noodles are made. The statue is conspicuously worn down, its surface polished by time.

Just to the right of Jizo, two squatting *rakan* seem to be eating their stone noodles. Legend has it that in the Edo period a soba merchant from Asakusa offered a daily plateful to the priest of a nearby temple, who turned out to be an incarnation of Jizo.

The merchant's family was henceforth protected from the afflictions and epidemics of the early 19th century, giving rise to this practice that continued after the temple was moved (see below).

NERIMA / ITABASHI / KITA

Eleven Tajima-san temples

The short impasse leading into the eleven temples of the Tajima-san complex offers a momentary escape from the bustle of Toshima-en, the largest amusement park in the east of the city.

The temples have a certain architectural and photogenic coherence, but are still determinedly modern, fulfilling a more spiritual than touristic role.

These eleven temples of the Jodo-shu sect, subsidiaries of Seiganji temple, were originally located in Asakusa-Tajimamachi (today Nishi-Asakusa, near Asakusa), but had to be moved here in 1928 after the destruction wrought by the 1923 earthquake. They were rearranged alongside the impasse. Seiganji itself was moved to Fuchu.

The Buddhist complex, very little used except by worshippers, over-looks a rather grand cemetery, also moved after the earthquake. An imposing Buddha statue dominates the entrance. Many Edo person-alities are buried here, such as Ikenaga Doun[1] in the Juyoin temple section and the herbalist Ono Ranzan[2] in the Kojoin temple section.

NEARBY
Shingyoji
(8)

Curvaceous temple

Just to the east of the Tajimasan complex, Shingyo-ji at 2-12-11 Nerima was founded in the 1920s. The main building, echoing the shapes of South Asian temples with its semi-floral curves, dates from the 1950s. It was inspired by the unique style of Hongan-ji at Tsukuji.

Toshima-en and its castle

Not many people know that Toshima-en amusement park (としまえん) stands on the site of the medieval Nerima Castle (練馬城), built around the middle of the 14th century, of which no physical trace remains. The dungeon has been replaced by the Hydropolis slide. The castle belonged to the Toshima clan, as did Shakujii Castle (石神井城), which led to a number of archaeological excavations in the heart of the lovely Shakujii Park.cœur du très agréable parc de Shakujii.

---

[1] 池永道雲, 1674–1737. Great calligrapher and seal engraver.
[2] 小野蘭山, 1729–1810. Herbalist and naturalist, who in 1803 completed a major compendium that earned him the nickname "Linnaeus of the East".

OBSERVATORY AT NERIMA TOWN HALL ⑨

A fine view over your coffee

6-12-1 Toyotamakita, Nerima-ku (東京都練馬区豊玉北 6-12-1)
10-minute walk from Nerima station (練馬), Seibu-Ikebukuro, Seibu-Yurakucho or Toei Oedo lines
Open 9am–9.30pm, closed 29 December to 4 January and fourth Sunday of the month

Dominating the south side of Nerima station, Nerima town hall (練馬区役所) is one of the few tall buildings in the ward. The 20th floor has an observatory and café, often empty.

The splendid panorama from the observation decks of Tokyo Metropolitan Government Building No. 1 in Shinjuku is quite well known. The view from the Nerima building, although not so high as Shinjuku, is just as interesting. It's also free.

Nerimaru, the radish mascot of Nerima, points the way along the observatory corridors. Another notable attraction is a different perspective of the heart of the city, including Shinjuku's skyscrapers (which you can only glimpse from Shinjuku!) in silhouette. If your luck's in, and the weather not too humid, there's also a stunning view of the other side of Mount Fuji.

Although one or two high buildings obstruct the view, they happen to be in less interesting directions, unless you want to see the outer suburbs of Saitama.

NEARBY

Toshima-Benzaiten ⑩
A shrine to water...with no water

The street north of Nerima station, Benten-dori, is lined with some little old-style shops, Showa atmosphere guaranteed.

Amidst all this it's easy to miss the path to Toshima-Benzaiten (豊島弁財天), a small shrine wedged between a coin laundry and a pub at 2-2 Nerima. Benzaiten, a Japanese Buddhist deity of Hindu origin (known as Sarasvati) and one of the seven gods of good luck, is often identified with Ichikishimahime the water goddess in the syncretism between Buddhism and Shinto. Yet there's no river nearby.

In fact, there once was a spring here that ran into the Shakujiigawa. The stream is now underground, but the easy-to-find lane that winds north of the shrine along twisting alleys follows its route.

The Shakujiigawa was an essential part of the defences of Nerima Castle where it used to stand at Toshima-en Park, so naturally all due respect was paid to the nearby watercourses.

EKODA'S FUJIZUKA

Tokyoite version of Mount Fuji

1-59-2 Kotakemachi, Nerima-ku (東京都練馬区小竹町 1-59-2)
2-minute walk from Ekoda station (江古田), Seibu-Ikebukuro line
Can be visited any time, but admission only three times a year: January 1 to 3,
July 1 and second Saturday in September

Just at the north exit of Ekoda station, in the precincts of the Asama shrine, a *torii* leads to a wooded hill just 8 metres high. Known as the Fujizuka of Ekoda (江古田の富士塚), this artificial mound dating from the first half of the 19th century is one of Tokyo's few few remaining examples of a *Fujizuka* – small replicas of Mount Fuji to allow those who can't cope with the climb to make an alternative pilgrimage.

Nowadays, although the mound can be viewed any time, climbing it is only allowed three times a year: from 1 to 3 January for the *hatsumode* (first Shinto shrine visit of Japanese New Year), on 1 July (corresponding to the opening of the climbing season of the real Mount Fuji) and on the second Saturday in September (annual festival of the shrine). During the few days when the ascent is allowed, a succession of aspiring climbers appears, but fortunately the crowd isn't as dense as at the top of Mount Fuji. The relative ease with which you can now climb the mountain explains the fairly limited demand for an alternative.

Other Tokyo Fujizukas

Several Fujizukas of varying sizes are scattered around the city. Ekoda is one of the best preserved, along with those at the Onoterusaki shrine at Shitaya, near Ueno, and at the Fuji-Asama shrine in Takamatsu district (Toshima ward). Ekoda is certainly not the highest, as some of the Fujizukas of the twenty-three wards are around 12 metres – one in Fuchu city even reaches 30 metres. The Fujizukas are a late 18th century phenomenon that peaked in the 19th century, limited to the Kanto region and Tokyo itself. Most of them were built in the Edo period, when belief in the divinity of the mountain was growing in popularity.

As climbing the real Mount Fuji is now much easier, the Fujizukas have lost their point, especially as you must be able to see Mount Fuji from the top of a Fujizuka for the pilgrimage to succeed, and the height of modern Tokyo buildings now obscures the view of the mountain.

On the same principle, alternative pilgrimage sites developed in Europe during the Renaissance for those who couldn't go to Jerusalem, or wouldn't go for security reasons. See *Secret Tuscany* in this series of guides.

TOKIWADAI AND ITS CULS-DE-SAC ⑫

Serenity in the north-west of the city

1 and 2 Tokiwadai, Itabashi-ku (東京都板橋区常盤台 1 and 2)
Tokiwadai station (ときわ台), Tobu-Tojo line
Accessible 24/7

A few stops from Ikebukuro on the Tobu-Tojo line, in the heart of Itabashi ward, Tokiwadai (常盤台) is a little-known oasis of chic individual residences. They were designed in 1935 by Komiya Kenichi[1] for Tobu Railways, the real-estate developer and rail operator in the area. The residences are grouped around a junction at the north side of the station, with wooded, curving streets where each can guard its privacy, footpaths and five culs-de-sac. You might be forgiven for thinking you were in the garden suburb of Den-en-Chofu. These are in fact the only "authentic culs-de-sac" planned as such in Tokyo. They share one feature: no vehicles, pedestrian access only.

The urban plan strictly specified the amount of land to be allocated for residential use, shopping and schools. The development was originally aimed at the middle classes but later attracted higher-income buyers. Many of the houses built at the time (a blend of traditional Japanese and "Western" style) have gradually disappeared in successive waves of urban regeneration, but some original buildings have survived, such as Teito kindergarten at 1-6-2 Tokiwadai and a private residence at 2-9-5. And if you're really curious, a building that used to be a photographic studio has been moved to the Edo-Tokyo Open Air Architectural Museum at Koganei.

Even without its historic buildings, the small development of Tokiwadai exudes a serenity unique to the north-west of the city, and the community envisaged by Komiya Kenichi now seems to be firmly rooted in the urban fabric. Unlike the south-west of Tokyo, the contrast between the neighbourhood and its surroundings is particularly striking. In all directions around Tokiwadai, you'll find the typical urban landscape of the northern districts, with their large impersonal mansions, small houses making the best of a miniscule plot, *pachinko* parlours and *combini* stores.

This oasis is now in danger of being engulfed, as shown by posters on the walls of several houses denouncing the construction of large residential complexes.

---

[1] 小宮賢一, *1911-1990. Architect and urban planner.*

DAGASHI-YA GAME MUSEUM ⑬

Masterpieces from the old days

17-8 Miyamotocho, Itabashi-ku (東京都板橋区宮本町 17-8)
10-minute walk from Itabashi-Honcho station (板橋本町), Toei subway
Mita line
Open 10am–7pm Saturday and Sunday, 2pm–7pm weekdays; closed Tuesday
and Wednesday (open if those days are public holidays)

In the golden age, even in the 1980s, *dagashi* vendors were everywhere in the country, on every street corner, at the heart of the social life of Japanese children. They would tempt the children to spend their hard-earned pocket money on cakes, candies and games.

Housed in the premises of Kontamura municipal centre at Itabashi, the Dagashi-ya Game Museum (駄菓子屋ゲーム博物館), a retro-style arcade, offers to plunge you back into that ambience. It has around fifty slot machines and medal games (in working order) from the 1970s and 80s, the screenless ancestors of video and pinball arcade games.

Great care is taken to introduce visitors to the special atmosphere of the time: the original machines are there to exchange your coins for medals, and of course you can buy *dagashi*. There are also some old *Gachagacha* mangas at the entrance to retrieve toys from the grabbing-claw machines.

Although the museum isn't really an arcade and isn't really a museum, it allows you to step back a few decades easily and lightheartedly.

FOOTPATH OF KIRIGAOKA *DANCHI*

On the old railway tracks to Kirigaoka ammunition depot

Near 3-17 Kirigaoka, Kita-ku (東京都北区桐ヶ丘 3-17)
20 minutes from Akabane station (赤羽), JR Saikyo, Keihin-Tohoku, Takasaki, Utsunomiya or Shonan-Shinjuku lines; Akabane-Toeijutaku bus stop (赤羽都営住宅); Kokusai-Kogyo lines 赤50, 赤51, 赤53, 赤56, 赤57 from Akabane station

I n the vast *danchi* of Kirigaoka just behind the hexagonal gym building, opposite the tennis courts, a footpath leads into an undulating green corridor. It's curiously decorated as if it were covered with railway sleepers.

The footpath actually follows the route of a former military freight line, which connected various facilities before the war (see also p. 150).

This winding path goes as far as Akabane Nature Observation Park, also on former military terrain taken over by the Japan Self-Defense Forces (自衛隊) in the 1950s. Rehabilitated as a nature park in 1999, it aims to replicate the area's natural environment before human intervention – a noble and very ambitious undertaking.

KOYAMA-SHUZO BREWERY ⑮

The last sake brewery in town

26-10 Iwabuchi-Machi, Kita-ku (東京都北区岩淵町 26-10)
5-minute walk from Akabane-Iwabuchi station (赤羽岩淵), Tokyo metro
Nanboku line
Tours and tastings organized once a week (usually on Wednesdays) – booking
required, by fax at 03-3902-3453 or online at www.koyamashuzo.co.jp/kura.
php

At Exit 3 of Akabane-Iwabuchi station, Route 122, also known as Kita-Hondori, runs north to Saitama through the Iwabuchi-Machi neighbourhood.

Along this road, at 38-23, a vaguely mushroom-shaped building might remind those with a good imagination of Moto-Azabu Hills tower blocks. The building is the main office of Keiaisha, a leading vehicle recycling company.

On the other side of the road behind a brewery, at 26-9 just before the Shin-Arakawa-Ohashi Bridge, is a small white sake store, Koyama-Shuten (小山酒店).

Koyama-Shuzo (小山酒造), which produces *Marushin-Masamune* (丸眞正宗) sake, is the only remaining sake brewery within Tokyo's twenty-three wards and uses water pumped over 100 metres underground.

Tours and tastings lasting 40 minutes are organized once a week (usually on Wednesdays, booking required).

But even during the tour, the cellar is closed. You'll have to settle for a video of the manufacturing process followed by a tasting.

For sake lovers or the simply curious, produce from the nearby brewery is available in the Koyama-Shuten store (which despite its name is not run directly by Koyama-Shuzo). Closed Tuesdays and Wednesdays.

AKABANE HACHIMAN

Boyzband and Shinto

4-1-6 Akabanedai, Kita-ku (東京都北区赤羽台 4-1-6)
10-minute walk from Abakane station (赤羽), JR Saikyo, Keihin-Tohoku,
Takasaki, Utsunomiya or Shonan-Shinjuku lines

Just north of Akabane, enclosed by the Keihin-Tohoku tracks, above the Shinkansen high-speed rail network that enters a tunnel here, stands the Akabane Hachiman shrine (赤羽八幡神社) – otherwise known as the "Protector of the North" because of its position above the tracks and passengers. The Shinkansen train passing between the *torii* makes a good photo.

Curiously, worshippers who don't seem to be train spotters can frequently be seen – mainly young women, which is rather surprising

at a Shinto site in a neighbourhood not notably popular with Tokyo's fashionistas.

The reason for the shrine's popularity among this particular group deserves an explanation. Fengshui plays a major role in this and the shrine offers *omamori* talismans for the twenty-year period Fengshui *Kagen-8-un* (下元8運), between 2004 and 2024, with a rather special design.

These talismans make graphic use of the figure 8, that period's lucky number, placed on its side to form the sign for infinity. As this symbol is also used by the boy band *Kanjani-8*, the link was soon made.

So the shrine is high on the must-visit list of Kanjani fans ("eighters"), who snap up the *omamori*. The shrine has latched onto this phenomenon, not missing the fact that the band was launched in 2004. That can't be a coincidence.

ARAKAWA MUSEUM OF AQUA

All about the Arakawa

5-41-1 Shimo, Kita-ku (東京都北区志茂 5-41-1)
10-minute walk from Akabane-Iwabuchi station (赤羽岩淵), Tokyo metro Nanboku line
Open 9.30am–5pm (closes at 5.30pm July to September) every day except Monday – if a public holiday falls on a Monday the museum is open, but closed the following day; closed for year-end holidays

Learn all about the river that waters the east of the capital in the Arakawa Museum of Aqua (荒川知水資料館), one of Tokyo's most interesting small free museums, dedicated to the Arakawa just opposite the old lock (see p. 146).

The museum is very detailed, and the first floor even has a few aquariums with fish from the river ecosystem.

The various exhibitions are well done: the history of the river, its place in the city and the challenge of building the canal and its historic lock are presented with passion and precision. At the weekend, volunteer guides are on site, complementing the exhibitions with their anecdotes and explanations.

Unsurprisingly, given its location and the specific topic it addresses, the museum is only rarely used except by schoolchildren.

But a visit is highly recommended for a better understanding of how rivers have shaped (and are continuing to shape) Tokyo, particularly towards the east.

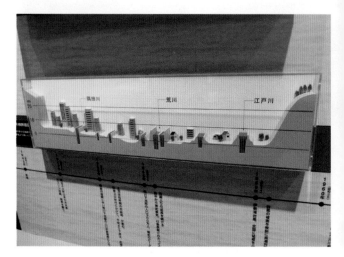

The Arakawa: a river by any other name

Curiously, the Arakawa doesn't flow through the neighbourhood of that name. When Arakawa ward was set up in 1945, the Sumida River was known as the Arakawa and gave its name to the new administrative division that it demarcated.

The downstream section of the river now called the *Arakawa* (荒川 – Violent River), which runs into Tokyo Bay, is actually a flood-control channel built between 1913 and 1930.

Prior to this work, the historic Arakawa was (as the name implies) extremely capricious.

The great flood of 1910, which triggered the launch of the project, had submerged the Shitamachi ("low town") neighbourhood, leaving more than 1,300 dead.

The colossal task of excavating the channel, delayed by the Great Kanto Earthquake of 1923, claimed another thirty victims. The metropolis was less extensive at the time and the channel was laid out across fields, affecting only some thousand homes.

The resulting artificial watercourse of 22 kilometres, and often over 500 metres wide, runs right through north-east Tokyo.

Although it was initially called the *Arakawa Hosuiro* (荒川放水路 – Arakawa Floodway), people gradually accepted it and in 1965 it became officially known as the main bed of the Arakawa, while the old river took the name Sumida.

Today, the embankments of the Arakawa are mainly landscaped parks to reduce the flood risk; they offer a breath of fresh air to the east of the city.

Few guess that Tokyo's widest river isn't a natural watercourse.

IWABUCHI LOCKS

⑱

At the source of the Sumida River

5-41 Shimo, Kita-ku (東京都北区志茂 5-41)
10-minute walk from Akabane-Iwabuchi station (赤羽岩淵), Tokyo metro
Nanboku line
Open 24/7

Two magnificent locks, one red and one blue, overlook the Sumida flowing to its confluence with the Arakawa.

The new Iwabuchi lock (新岩淵水門) is often just referred to as the blue lock (青水門), logically enough. This imposing, elegant structure has been open since 1982 and is sometimes illuminated at night in the school holidays.

A few metres upstream, the old lock of Iwabuchi (旧岩淵水門; the red lock) is permanently open.

Just down from the lock itself, a promenade along the banks gives an idea of the level the water reached during various historical incidents, justifying the apparent vast scale of the surrounding embankments. The old lock was built between 1916 and 1924. Now gradually listing into the water, it's no longer in use or indeed in working order, but it's still a fine piece of engineering from the Taisho era.

NEARBY
Nakanoshima ⑲
Mowing the grass on a haunted island

Walk across the short stretch of river spanned by the old lock to reach the narrow island of Nakanoshima. Here you'll find a stele commemorating the highlights of an annual grass-mowing competition held on the banks of the Arakawa from 1938 to 1943, and a startling modern statue poetically called *Tsuki wo iru* (月を射る – Targeting the Moon).

Incidentally, the old lock and this small island are thought to be haunted by the spirits of those drowned in the Arakawa, caught for ever in the lock. A fisherman was struck down by lightning on Nakanoshima in early August 2013, for those who doubt that the place is accursed. Both island and lock are accessible at night.

KYU-FURUKAWA TEIEN GARDENS ㉚

Magnificent Western-style residence on the edge of a plateau

1-27-39 Nishigahara, Kita-ku (東京都北区西ヶ原 1-27-39)
5-minute walk from Nishigahara station (西ヶ原), Tokyo metro Nanboku line
Open 9am–5pm daily, closed 29 December to 1 January

Kyu-Furukawa Teien gardens (旧古河庭園), near Nishigahara station, are for once not the former site of an Edo noble's residence, but of a peony garden that statesman Mutsu Munemitsu[1] had converted at the time of the Meiji Restoration. He died there in 1897.

The estate then passed into the hands of Baron Furukawa Toranosuke,[2] the man behind the diversification of the powerful Furukawa *zaibatsu*,[3] who built a large Westernized house in 1917 to the plans of London architect Josiah Conder.[4]

The gardens were opened to the public 1956 and the house was restored in the 1980s. Standing on the Musashino plateau, the house now overlooks a European garden with a Japanese garden below. The very pleasant grounds are beautifully maintained.

Sit on a bench with a coffee, gaze over the estate and escape the bustle of the city for a while. The surrounding gardens are also very restful.

[1] 陸奥宗光, *1844–1897, Meiji Restoration politician, diplomat and minister, negotiator of the Treaty of Shimonoseki that ended the first Sino-Japanese War (1894–1895).*
[2] 古河虎之助, *1887-1940.*
[3] 古河財閥, *one of the leading pre-war industrial and financial conglomerates (zaibatsu), dismantled during the Allied Occupation, precursor of Fujitsu IT multinational among other companies.*
[4] *1852-1920.*

MOUNT ASUKA PLAQUE (21)

Lowest mountain in Tokyo Metropolis

1-1-3 Oji, Kita-ku (東京都北区王子 1-1-3)
5 minutes from Oji station (王子), JR Keihin-Tohoku line; Tokyo metro
Nanboku line; Toei Arakawa streetcar
Park open 24/7, Ascargo open 10am–4pm daily; closed 29 December to
3 January and for maintenance 10am–12 noon first Thursday of the month

Kita ward claims (very seriously and officially) the title of lowest mountain in Tokyo Metropolis for Mount Asuka, which, at only 25.4 metres, is only a few centimetres lower than Mount Atago's 25.7 metres (see p. 44).

Although the Geospatial Information Authority of Japan (GSI) hasn't included Mount Asuka in the list of peaks in Tokyo Metropolis, citing lack of space on the maps, the ward has still installed a plaque noting its height above sea level.

The difference between the lowest and the highest point is only 17.5 metres, crossed by the monorail of Asukayama Park (aka Ascargo). Since 2009, this amazing automated cabin with sixteen places (six seated) has carried passengers free up the short path (48 metres) between the road and the summit of Mount Asuka – it takes about 2 minutes. The cabin is air-conditioned and spacious – all mod cons.

The mount lies in Asukayama, one of the first parks in the city. Established at the same time as Ueno Park but much less well-known (although very pleasant and, like its cousin, a cherry blossom high spot), it extends along the rails south of Oji station.

The park has a memorial to industrialist Shibusawa Eiichi,[1] together with his home and library, both contemporary buildings classed as Important Cultural Properties.

---

[1] 渋沢栄一, *1840–1931. Businessman and founder of a number of companies, institutes and universities, many of which still exist today. Shibusawa is regarded as one of the fathers of modern Japanese capitalism.*

REMAINS OF JUJO MUNITIONS FACTORY

Ammunition for the Zero fighters

Kita-ku Central Library
1-2-5 Jujodai, Kita-ku (東京都北区十条台 1-2-5)
15 minutes from Oji station (王子), JR Keihin-Tohoku line; Tokyo metro
Nanboku line; Toei Arakawa streetcar; or 10 minutes from Jujo station (十条),
JR Saikyo line
Open 9am–8pm Monday to Saturday, 9am–5pm Sundays and public holidays;
closed the first, third and fifth Mondays of the month and the fourth Thursday
of the month, and December 29 to January 4

Kita-ku Central Library (北区立中央図書館), opened in 2008 in the north-east of Chuo Park, has a café with a very pleasant terrace bordered by a brick façade. These red bricks are the remains of Building No. 275 of the Jujo factory of the Tokyo First Arsenal of the Japanese Army (東京第一陸軍造兵廠・十条工場), which made ammunition notably for the famous Zero fighter planes. The building stood inside the walls of the base of the nearby Japan Self-Defense Forces (JSDF),[1] who visited Kita ward. The other buildings from the time of the arsenal were destroyed when the base was renovated.

First arsenal

The former site of the arsenal's Jujo factory still structures the whole urban landscape around Chuo Park.

A cartridge factory established in 1905 during the Russo-Japanese War became, over the years, one of Tokyo's main military production centres. The site of around 100 hectares covered in particular (but not only) what is now Chuo Park and the Jujo site of the JSDF.

In its heyday, the factory had around 40,000 employees and produced ammunition, radios and explosives.

Despite repeated attacks on Takinogawa (bombed a dozen times), and the strategic importance of this target, the factory escaped relatively lightly.

The site was occupied by the US military at the end of the war. The northern section was returned to Japan in 1958, which opened the above-mentioned JSDF base.

Kita cultural centre: former headquarters of first arsenal munitions factory

In the centre of Chuo Park, the elegant white building with its Western-style architecture is the Central Park Cultural Center (中央公園文化センター).

Built in 1930, the building was the headquarters of the munitions factory of the first arsenal before and during the war.

After the war, it became the Pacific base of the United States Army Security Agency (ASA). A US military hospital was opened there in 1968 and the building became one of the symbols of Japanese civilian opposition to the Vietnam War, with almost daily demonstrations. In 1971, administration of the land was returned to Japan. An old boiler from the factory is displayed on the east side of the building.

Right next to the arsenal site is the new campus of the Lycée Français International de Tokyo, opened in 2012 on the former site of Ikebukuro commercial and vocational school after several years of negotiations.

This site was apparently occupied after the war by a knitwear manufacturer.

---

[1] *Japan Self-Defense Force, Japanese Defense Forces (自衛隊).*

COMMEMORATING THE SECOND ARSENAL'S POWDER CRUSHER

Remains of the imperial army

1-10 Kaga, Itabashi-ku (東京都板橋区加賀 1-10)
10 minutes from Shin-Itabashi station (新板橋), Toei subway Mita line

An imposing powder crusher (圧磨機圧), imported from Belgium in the late 19th century and a relic of the military past around Itabashi, has been converted into a stele that stands behind Higashi-Itabashi gymnasium at 1-10 Kaga.

The crusher mixed saltpeter, charcoal and sulphur by means of a mechanism set in motion by the waters of the Shakujii River. The workings of the old crusher are explained on a small information panel.

The curious monument is now dedicated to Sawa Tarozaemon,[1] founder of the arsenal.

A military man sent to Europe by the shogunate to study the manufacture of gunpowder, Sawa participated in the founding of the ephemeral Republic of Ezo alongside the shogunate forces opposing the Meiji Restoration.

Tokyo's second arsenal

The country estate that was second home to the powerful Maeda clan of Kaga covered around 72 hectares in the Edo period (more than today's Yoyogi Park); it was converted for military use on the Meiji Restoration.

From 1876 an army artillery depot was installed there, then in 1940 a large ammunition production centre with the huge Itabashi factory of Tokyo's second arsenal of the imperial army.

The location near the Shakujii gave direct access to the city's waterways.

The bed of the Shakujii, tributary of the Sumida, is now managed to limit the risk of flooding. Because it's so narrow, a gorge several metres deep has had to be dredged.

The residence of the Maeda clan is commemorated by a rather non-descript pillar in the small Kaga Park.

It's a reminder of the great days of the shogunate, when the property covered much of the neighbourhoods of 1 and 2 Kaga, and 3 and 4 Itabashi. The hill in the park is artificial: a vestige of the land-scaped garden of the residence, which has lost all its past splendour. The area, and therefore the second arsenal, extended to the level of the Saikyo railway line.

NEARBY
Noguchi Institute   ㉔
Military remains

The Noguchi Institute (野口研究所), a biology research institute found-ed in 1941, was installed after the war in 1946 on the site of the second arsenal along the Shakujiigawa. The institute, at 1-8-1 Kaga, can be visited (only on reservation) to discover other military remains from the time of the arsenal, such as a concrete pipe to test ammunition. The pipe can be seen from the outside of the institute.

In Kaga Park, next to the institute, the wall of bricks and mortar was part of a test target.

---

1 澤太郎左衛門, *1834-1898.*

REMADENS OF ITABASHISHUKU

REMAINS OF ITABASHISHUKU

REMAINS OF ITABASHISHUKU (25)

First stop on the Nakasendo route

Near 47-12 Nakajuku, Itabashi-ku (東京都板橋区仲宿 47-12)
10 minutes from Itabashi-Kuyakushomae station (板橋区役所前),
Toei subway Mita line

The strange plain black stone next to a Life supermarket at 47-12 Nakajuku marks the site of Itabashishuku's *honjin*, the heart of the first *shukuba* of the historic Nakasendo route where the feudal lords rested on their way to and from Edo.

Itabashihoncho station is at the north end of the *shukuba*. The Nakasendo passed by here, just east of the modern wide Nakasendo, along a busy street lined with small traditional shops that are worth strolling through.

Itabashishuku covered over 2 kilometres from north to south. The

centre, Nakajuku, was transformed with the opening of Itabasahi station, much farther south, in an attempt to attract travellers.

At the end of the Meiji era, having been partially destroyed in a serious fire in 1884, Nakajuku became one of the capital's great pleasure centres.

Looking around, you can still see some vintage brick walls (brick being more fire-resistant) between the shops, relics of the old Itabashishuku. At 40 Nakajuku, there is even an almost intact Taisho rice shop, now occupied by an estate agent. The temple in the back alley, Hensho-ji, used to be a stable in the Edo era.

Stops on the Edo routes

The Five Routes crossing the country were introduced in the Edo period. They began at a "zero" point at Nihonbashi and allowed the feudal lords, especially those in the provinces, to comply with the *sankin kotai* (参勤交代). This system, inaugurated by the Tokugawa shogunate, obliged the feudal lords to reside in the capital Edo for several months a year. When they returned to their fiefs, they were required to leave their families in Edo. Other minor roads ran farther into the countryside, but these five were the key arteries of economic and cultural exchanges. They were punctuated by rest stops, *shukuba* (宿場), allowing travellers – and, of course, the lords and their retainers – to rest, and giving the shogunate the means of controlling the flow of goods and people around the country. At the heart of these *shukuba* was the *honjin* (本陣), an inn where the lord was put up for the night. The first four *shukuba* on the roads to Edo did in fact mark the boundaries of the city. To the south, Shinagawa (see p. 61) opened the Tokaido, perhaps the country's most important road, which linked Edo to Kyoto via the Pacific coast. To the northwest, Itabashi (p. 154), on the Nakasendo, also led to Kyoto, but via the mountains. To the west, Naito-Shinjuku, the most recent Edo *shukuba* (p. 168), was the first stop on the Koshu-kaido, leading to the province of Kai (now Yamanashi prefecture). Finally, the Nikko-kaido, which branched off onto the Oshu-kaido near Utsunomiya, led northwards. Senju (p. 196) was the first stop common to both roads. With the arrival of the railways at the end of the 19th century, and the end of the feudal processions, these four staging posts have lost their importance and have slowly but surely gone downhill. However, there are still some interesting traces of what were major centres of the Edo economy.

ENKIRI ENOKI

Help in quitting smoking or dumping your partner

18 Honmachi, Itabashi-ku (東京都板橋区本町 18)
10-minute walk from Itabashi-Honmachi station (板橋本町), Toei subway
Mita line
Accessible 24/7

Along Itabashi-shuku, at 18 Honmachi, a species of tree has been the object of a rather special cult: Enkiri Enoki (縁切榎 – Hackberry of Separation). It's said that the tree will grant the wishes of anyone who wishes to cut their ties with someone or something.

To stop smoking or drinking, dump an unwanted partner or rid yourself of a clingy colleague, this is the place.

The texts of the *emas* lined up in the tiny enclosure show that visitors are often at their wits' end. Here it's not a question of seeking victory or world peace; the only aim is to escape from an ex-partner, a job, illness, from anything and everything, as quickly as possible.

In popular tradition, pieces of bark were crushed and infused to make a drink.

Today's hackberrys (their bark protected from unwelcome harvesting) are third-generation, planted on a slightly different spot to their illustrious ancestor. A piece of the bark of the second-generation tree has been preserved in a commemorative stone. The original tree burned down in the Meiji era.

The hackberry was one of the healthy trees of a shrine dedicated to the Tenma goddesses.[1]

The only hackberry in a row of elms – which some believe to be the spot where Jikigyo Miroku[2] wished to bid farewell to his wife and children before ascending Mount Fuji, and others think is why the tree is associated with separation – is a source of controversy.

The site's (poor) reputation is so ingrained that a detour had to be built when Princess Chikako de Kazu[3] travelled the Nakasendo route to Edo in 1861 to marry the 14th shogun; this was to avoid her passing the tree of ill omen.

---

[1] *Guardian deities in Buddhism.*
[2] 食行身禄, *1671–1733, an Edo monk who developed a belief centred on Mount Fuji.*
[3] 和宮親子内親王, *1846–1877, often called Princess Kazunomiya, daughter of Ninko, 120th emperor.*

Shibuya / Shinjuku

WASEDA EL DORADO

Catalan modernism at Waseda

517 Waseda Tsurumakicho, Shinjuku-ku (東京都新宿区早稲田鶴巻町 517)
3-minute walk from Waseda station (早稲田), Tokyo metro Toza line
Interior closed to non-residents

Waseda El Dorado, with a barber shop on the first floor, is a small five-storey residential building erected in 1984 by Von Jour Caux and his Art Complex near the main Waseda campus.

The exterior might remind you of Gaudí's work in Barcelona, although it's even more eccentric. The façade with its clockface knows no restraint. Angular, curved and lavishly decorated, its many absurd details are astonishing. Masks and mysterious sculptures of bodies are set into the walls, and opulent wrought-iron railings with curved motifs complete the ensemble.

Visitors and residents are greeted at the entrance by an ornate mosaic showing a devil sticking out his tongue. The walls of what is probably the hallway are also decorated with brightly coloured mosaics. Everything here is curved and rather organic, rich in colour and stained glass. Down the hall, a huge arm hangs from the ceiling, the last big surprise before the residents' area. El Dorado is still a residential block, so you can't go any farther.

For more on Von Jour Caux, see p. 94.

TSUMAMI-KANZASHI MINI MUSEUM

Folded decorations

Hills Ishida Apt 401, 4-23-28 Takadanobaba, Shinjuku-ku (東京都新宿区高田馬場 4-23-28 ヒルズ ISHIDA 401号)
2-minute walk from Takadanobaba station (高田馬場), JR Yamanote line;
Tokyo metro Tozai or Seibu Shinjuku lines
Open 10am–5pm, Wednesday and Saturday only

Tsumami-Kanzashi Mini Museum (つまみかんざし博物館), in a refurbished apartment, is devoted to the subtle and little-known craft of making ornamental hairpins using dyed silk pieces folded and arranged by hand.

Nowadays mastered only by a handful of enthusiastic artisans, *tsu-mami-kanzashi* is a 200-year-old Tokyo variant of *kanzashi*. In 1993 Ishida Takeshi,[1] an artisan himself and descendant of a kanzashi creator, decided to open a small home workshop now recognized as a "mini museum" in Shinjuku ward.

Although there is a lift, it's better to climb the stairs to the fourth-floor museum to see some noticeboards on the art of *kanzashi*.

With any luck, the master of the house will come and welcome you and answer any questions.

Although the small permanent exhibition includes only a dozen works on a glass shelf, that's already enough to discover and appreciate the level of detail in these creations. In addition, Takeshi sometimes shows his work in department stores (information available at the museum).

There are no direct sales at the museum, but you can order *kan-zashis* online. Courses are held regularly for anyone wishing to initiate themselves into this elegant craft. To date, the workshop isn't open to the public.

[1] 石田毅司, *1959-.*

HAKONE-YAMA

In the hills above the city

Toyama, Shinjuku-ku (東京都新宿区戸山) in Toyama-koen
15-minute walk from Waseda station (早稲田), Tokyo metro Tozai or Nishi-
Shinjuku lines (西新宿); Toei subway Oedo line; Tokyo metro Fukutoshin station
Accessible 24/7

Hakone-Yama (箱根山), south of Toyama Park, is at 44.6 metres the highest point of the Yamanote hills. The view from the summit is pleasant although unexceptional. In the background, the skyscrapers of Shinjuku emerge above the trees in the park.

A simple plaque at the top gives the altitude. The artificial hill was constructed in the Edo period by Tokugawa Mitsutomo[1] of the Owari branch of the Tokugawa clan, using earth excavated from a pond at the heart of a pleasure garden replicating the Tokaido route (Edo to Kyoto). The hill was showcased as the Tokaido's Mount Hakone.

A monument at the foot of the hill commemorates the military school that occupied much of the park before the war.

The hexagonal bandstand used for the school music division's outdoor concerts is still there.

The United Church of Christ in Japan at Toyama, at the foot of Hakone-Yama, is also a kindergarten. The church was built in 1950 after the closure of the military school on the site of the officers' mess, bricks from which can still be seen in the foundations.

Human remains below the International Research Center for Infectious Diseases

In 1989, during construction of the new Research Center next to the park, the remains of around a hundred bodies were discovered. The fact that this was the site of the military medical school triggered controversy, especially since analysis revealed that the apparently non-Japanese bodies were the victims of medical experiments. The infamous Unit 731[2] that operated under the auspices of the school's infectious diseases laboratories, the source of these human remains, were widely reported.

In 2006 a former military nurse confirmed that she had buried body parts after the Japanese surrender in 1945. Further excavations in the park in 2011 led to no new discoveries but attracted much attention.

---

[1] 徳川光友, *1625–1700.*
[2] *Manchuria military unit in charge of the development of biological weapons.*

ICHIGAYA FISH CENTER

④

Fishing in the moat of Edo Castle

1-1 Ichigayamachi, Shinjuku-ku (東京都新宿区市谷町 1-1)
2-minute walk from Ichigaya station (市ヶ谷), Tokyo metro Yurakucho
or Nanboku lines; Toei subway Shinjuku line; JR Chuo or Sobu lines
Open 9.30am–8pm weekdays, 9am–8pm weekends and public holidays

Not far from Sotobori Park, which runs along the former outer moat of Edo Castle, a few metres from the bustle of Ichigaya station,

Ichigaya Fish Center (市ヶ谷フィッシュセンターーIFC) has a tropical fish store and a selection of tanks, marine plants and items for the aquarium of all prices and styles.

But above all it helps you forget the trials and tribulations of daily life by running fishing sessions payable by the hour in (very) small pens in the castle moat.

You must release any fish caught, the aim being not to feed yourself but to take a break and relax through something less demanding than karaoke. Children or the less confident can stick to the goldfish.

NAITO-SHINJUKU DIORAMA

At the western entrance to the city

22 San-ei-cho, Shinjuku-ku (東京都新宿区三栄 町 22) in Shinjuku Historical Museum
5-minute walk from Yotsuya Sanchome station (四谷三丁目), Tokyo metro Marunouchi line
Open 9.30am–5.30pm daily, closed on second and fourth Mondays of the month – if a public holiday falls on a Monday the museum is open, but closed the following day; closed December 29 to January 3 and occasionally in December

Although three of the four historic rest stops (see p. 155) on the major routes from Edo, Itabashi (p. 154), Senju (p. 196) and Shinagawa (p. 61) have left a few traces in the city, the remains of Naito-Shinjuku (内藤新宿) are rarer.

The best way to gauge what the first *shukuba* on the Koshu-kaido route was like during the Edo period (in fact, the western entrance to the city at the time) is to visit Shinjuku Historical Museum. A very effective diorama on permanent display gives a snapshot of *shukuba* activity in an area that roughly extended from the crossroads at Yotsuya 4-chome, the checkpoint of Yotsuya Okido shogunate (四谷大木戸), to the crossroads of Shinjuku 3-chome, around today's Shinjuku-dori.

Unlike the other main *shukubas*, the Naito-Shinjuku establishment had some repercussions.

Historically, there were fewer travellers heading due west and back. Following a route encroaching on the territory of a Naito clan residence, the *shukuba* was first authorized in 1699, nearly a century after the creation of the shogunate (hence its name, *Shinjuku*, 新宿 – New Stop). It was abolished twenty years later, as there was no longer much demand, after sustaining two massive fires. Shinjuku was finally and definitively launched in 1772 and went from strength to strength, gradually becoming one of the major economic centres of the city. The vast building sites for the enlargement of Shinjuku-dori put an end to it.

NEARBY
Taiso-ji's Enma statue ⑥

Taiso-ji (太宗寺) lies a little north of the historic heart of the *shukuba* at 2-9-2 Shinjuku.

Within the temple grounds is a structure housing a very imposing 5-metre wooden statue of Enma, installed in 1814, known as the Enma of Naito-Shinjuku.

This is one of the few relics from the days of the Koshu-kaido rest stop. The body, however, dates from 1933. It was restored after serious damage during the Great Kanto Earthquake. Just beside Enma is a statue of Datsue-ba with a frightening expression.

GUNKAN HIGASHI-SHINJUKU

Building like a battleship

1-1-10 Okubo Shinjuku-ku (東京都新宿区大久保1-1-10)
5-minute walk from Higashi-Shinjuku station (東新宿), Tokyo metro
Fukutoshin line, Toei subway Oedo line
Public sometimes allowed inside

Designed in 1970 by Watanabe Yoji,[1] the Gunkan Higashi-Shinjuku building (GUNKAN 東新宿), formerly New Sky Building No. 3, is a 20th-century Japanese architectural monument that was almost lost.

Virtually abandoned until the 2000s, this battleship of a building was falling into ruin and under threat of demolition. A change of ownership and a top-to-bottom renovation saved the day and the building was finally reopened in 2011.

Gunkan Higashi-Shinjuku is now given over to shared office space and rented apartments. For those who have a good grasp of Japanese, several sessions of *Ajito of Scrap*[2] are held (or played) there most days.

The façade overlooking the thoroughfare of Shokuan-dori is very narrow, so you can't get an idea of the building in all its imposing grandeur. The ship, painted in blue-green, is more impressive seen from a distance – when you approach from the east and the concourse of Higashi-Shinjuku station, for example.

Note that the inside of the building (not freely accessible), which is particularly narrow, looks like the inside of a submarine because the layout admits very little natural light.

NEARBY ⑧

Toyama Heights, an ageing village in the Yamanote hills

A few minutes' walk from Gunkan Higashi-Shinjuku, the little-visited *danchi* of Toyama Heights (戸山ハイツ) is the largest social-housing complex run by Tokyo Metropolitan Government in the Yamanote hills. Toyama Heights is directly affected by the country's ageing phenomenon, as around half of the residents are over 65. Lonely deaths are not uncommon.

The situation is such that the complex has been described as *genkai-shuraku* (beyond the pale) in the heart of Yamanote. Walking around the various residential blocks is a reminder that Tokyo is not only a city for the young.

---

[1] 渡邊洋治, *1923–1983. Enlisted in 1944 in the Philippines as an amphibious assault soldier, an experience that would mark his architectural work, which is sometimes reminiscent of the metabolism movement.*
[2] *Role play game increasingly popular since the late 2000s, in which various clues are left in a closed room to allow participants to "escape".*

FOUNTAIN FOR HORSES AT THE EAST EXIT OF SHINJUKU

A fountain presented by London in 1906

3-38-1 Shinjuku, Shinjuku-ku (東京都新宿区新宿 3-38-1)
Shinjuku station (新宿), various lines

On the eastern square of the world's busiest station, under the glare of neon lights and the giant screen of Studio Alta, in one of the most crowded places in town, stands an unusual fountain that many residents have probably never even noticed. This drinking fountain for horses (馬水槽), in red marble, was donated by the municipal water distribution network of London in 1906.

The fountain was originally installed in front of Tokyo's former city hall at Yurakucho. It was moved to its present site in 1964 while preparations for the Olympic Games were in full swing. Horses drank from the upper of three sections, dogs and cats from the lower section, and a third source round the back lets passers-by quench their thirst too.

The fountain is no long in use and is now just a monument. No worries if you're thirsty – it's quite easy to find a drink in Shinjuku.

NEARBY
Mysterious pillars of Lumine Est ⑩
Abandoned station of Seibu-Shinjuku

The Lumine Est shopping centre occupies much of the structure of JR East Shinjuku station. Note the impressive reinforced pillars above the east exit (ground floor, near the ATMs), which seem a bit excessive.

The explanation for their robustness is related to the history of Seibu-Shinjuku line, which was initially to be extended as far as Shinjuku. The building that houses Lumine, opened in 1964, was designed to accommodate the platforms at the level of what is the second floor and these pillars were to bear their weight.

Unfortunately, the platforms in question proved too short to take the Seibu trains and support the burgeoning passenger numbers, and the plans were abandoned, leaving behind these pillars, neglected remains of faulty planning.

Seibu-Shinjuku line

The Murayama line, precursor of Seibu-Shinjuku, was opened in 1927 with a terminus at Takadanobaba (高田馬場). It was extended as far as the Seibu-Shinjuku temporary terminus in 1952, thus becoming the only private line to follow the Yamanote on part of its route. The line was renamed on that occasion.

When plans to extend the line to Shinjuku were abandoned in 1964, Seibu-Shinjuku terminus was found to be just far enough away from Shinjuku junction to break the momentum and make the line less attractive, while at the same time offering the opportunity to explore a lesser-known slice of western Tokyo.

RURIKOIN BYAKURENGEDO

A spectacular oasis of calm in the heart of Shinjuku

2-4-3 Yoyogi, Shibuya-ku (東京都渋谷区代々木 2-4-3)
5-minute walk from Shinjuku
Open 10am–6pm, closed Wednesday, guided tours at 11am and 2pm

In a narrow street just behind the Sunroute Plaza hotel, Rurikoin Byakurengedo temple (瑠璃光院白蓮華堂) is a remarkable concrete creation filled with the play of light and sound, all angles and curves. This is the Tokyo branch of the Jodo Shinshu sect's Komyo-ji.

The modern temple, opened in late September 2014, resembles a lotus flower irregularly pierced with windows, and serves as an ossuary among its other functions.

You can find peace in this exceptional place, away from the chaos of one of the most frenetic areas of the city, and even of the world. The interior of the temple, on six floors connected by lifts, combines elegance, simplicity and sophistication. One room features a reproduction of a Horyu-ji fresco, destroyed by fire in 1949. Plans are underway to expand the exhibition space.

From the main hall (本堂 – *hondo*, which has a reproduction of a fresco of China's Mogao grotto) to the vast adjoining multi-purpose salon (空ノ間 – *kuunoma*, with sound effects by Pierre Mariétan),[1] the temple is a series of architecturally perfect spiritual spaces.

It was designed by Amorphe Takeyama & Associates architectural design office around the concept of "non-action" (無為 – *mui*) and built by the Takenaka corporation.

[1] *1935 –. Swiss composer.*

PONIES IN YOYOGI MUNICIPAL PARK

Carrots for city ponies

4-1 Yoyogi-Kamizonocho, Shibuya-ku (東京都渋谷区代々木神園町 4-1)
2-minute walk from Sangubashi station (参宮橋), Odakyu line
Open 9am–5pm every day except Monday – if a public holiday falls on a
Monday the park is open, but closed the following day; closed for year-end
holidays

Right next to the vast green expanse of Yoyogi Park, an enclosure (渋谷区立代々木ポニー公園) gives children the chance to get close to half a dozen ponies in the heart of the city.

They can usually have a short ride (for about 60 metres), several times a day, except during the hot Tokyo midsummer (mid-July to mid-September) or the icy winter months of January and February. Anyway, they can always groom the ponies or feed them carrots.

The park opened in 2003, extending a one-off experiment by the Tokyo Riding Club next door, which now manages the park on behalf of the district.

For the record, the park is on the site of the former Yoyogi Municipal Park (渋谷区立代々木公園), under the jurisdiction of Shibuya ward, not to be confused with Yoyogi Park, which is run by Tokyo Metropolitan Government. In other words, until 2003 there were two Yoyogi Parks, one tiny and one huge, a short distance apart. There's only the one now.

HARAJUKU IMPERIAL DOCKS ⑬

A station for the emperor and his family

3-58 Sendagaya, Shibuya-ku (東京都渋谷区千駄ヶ谷 3-58)
Harajuku (原宿) JR Yamanote line
Inaccessible to the public but can be seen from Harajuku docks

In front of the green grounds of Meiji shrine, about 200 metres north of Harajuku public station in Yamanote, is a second station. This one is far less crowded, and for a good reason: the Imperial Quays (宮廷ホーム) of Harajuku are reserved for the imperial family.

The platforms were built in 1925 to allow Emperor Taisho (who often got around in a wheelchair because of his reputedly very fragile health) to discreetly take the train a little farther from the centre to go to one of his provincial retreats.

This station, unique of its kind in Tokyo's twenty-three wards, was regularly used by the Showa emperor Hirohito and Empress Kojun. The current emperor usually takes the "standard" Shinkansen from Tokyo or travels by car, so the docks are hardly ever used (at the time of writing, they hadn't been in use since May 2001). Using a private train interferes greatly with the schedules of other trains, and the present emperor is apparently aware of the negative impact this could have on the population, who are highly dependent on this form of transport.

The platforms are much shorter than those of a normal station, but there's no need to make them longer as not many passengers use them.

NEARBY
Sendagaya tunnel ⑭
The haunted tunnel

To facilitate access to the National Olympic Stadium during the 1964 Games, a tunnel was dug directly underneath the cemetery of Senjuin temple. During the construction work, the spirits of the deceased were unavoidably disturbed by moving the tombs, before reinstating them above the tunnel at the end of the work. Ever since there's been no lack of urban myths, taxi drivers who like to scare their fares, anecdotes on the radio – tales of ghosts, ectoplasm and long-haired spirits with who moan about their sufferings to the unwary who dare use the tunnel.

Despite all this, traffic is still quite heavy. A protected walkway lets brave pedestrians negotiate the 61-metre tunnel safely. The walls are covered with graffiti, a rare sight in Tokyo.

UPSTREAM ON THE SHIBUYA RIVER

Along hidden banks

Shibuya station (渋谷), JR Yamanote, Saikyo or Shonan Shinjuku lines; Tokyu Toyoko or Den-en-Toshi lines; Keio Inokashira line; Tokyo metro Hanzomon, Ginza or Fukutoshin lines
Accessible 24/7

The Shibuyagawa (渋谷川), concealed below the city streets along its first few kilometres, resurfaces with difficulty just south of Shibuya station to flow the 7 kilometres that separate it from Tokyo Bay. The district took its name from the river in reference to the reddish oxides colouring its waters.[1]

Except at times of heavy rain, the flow nowadays is very low or even zero. Covered in the early 1960s during preparations for the Olympics, the hidden upper stretch of the river, sometimes called Ondengawa, has left some interesting traces. Its source is historically inside Shinjuku-Gy-

oen Park. The river then crosses the Chuo line and heads south along the site of the National Olympic Stadium. The border between Shinjuku and Shibuya districts here follows the riverbed, which continues to the south-west, covered by a road that follows its bends before crossing the very fashionable Ura-Harajuku with its clothing shops. A mill with a waterwheel almost 7 metres in diameter, which stood near what is now 3-19-1 Jingumae until the Meiji era, is thought to have inspired Hokusai's painting, *Onden no suisha* (穏田の水車 – Waterwheel at Onden).

The river then flows directly under the famous Cat Street and towards the south, hence the winding nature of the road. Along its sinuous path are some original bridge piers indicating a crossing site, such as Ondenbashi at 5-11 Jingumae or Harajukubashi at 3-28 Jingumae. Closer to Shibuya, the river runs beneath a stretch of parkland at Miyashita-koen. The former East Building of Tokyu department store was built over the riverbed, and had no basement because of this.

Among the hidden tributaries of the Shibuyagawa, the Utagawa rises near Yoyogi-Uehara station and flows south-east a little west of Inokashira-dori. It was gradually covered over in the early 20th century as Shibuya was urbanized, before disappearing completely for the Olympics. Buildings 1 and 2 of the Shibuya Seibu department store are connected by footbridges, with the river flowing beneath.

The Utagawa was once diverted before it was covered over: its original course was below what is now the Center Gai shopping mall. The Utagawa meets the Shibuyagawa at the Miyamasubashi intersection. Major restoration work around Shibuya should make use of part of the river to create a new urban oasis.

Tokyo's hidden rivers

Whereas rapid urbanization has brought main thoroughfares and straight avenues to the alluvial plains on the east of the city, the rather more undulating land criss-crossed by watercourses makes the west side much less regular.

Apart from a few big rivers tamed in their concrete beds, a complex network of dozens of streams has gradually been buried to make way for the developing city. For curious strollers, some evidence of the historic river system remains on the surface, often in the form of long narrow parks or quirky alleys, following these sometimes forgotten watercourses. The Shibuyagawa is just one example of these – it's short and relatively easy to follow.

1 渋谷川 – *literally "River of the Ochre Valley".*

KOKUGAKUIN UNIVERSITY MUSEUM OF ARCHAEOLOGY

At the crossroads between Shinto and archaeology

4-10-28 Higashi, Shibuya-ku (東京都渋谷区東 4-10-28)
15-minute walk from Shibuya station (渋谷), JR Yamanote, Saikyo or Shonan Shinjuku lines; Tokyu Toyoko or Den-en-Toshi lines; Keio Inokashira line; Tokyo metro Hanzomon, Ginza or Fukutoshin lines
Open 10am–5pm, closed Sundays and public holidays; other occasional closures depending on academic requirements
Admission free

The private Kokugakuin University (國學院大學), a short walk from Shibuya, is an offshoot of the Koken Research Institute (皇典講究所), founded in the Meiji era and committed to Shinto research.

The university, whose bias is more literary and cultural than scientific or mathematical, still offers specialized courses in Shinto. It houses an archaeological museum with a focus on religion, an almost unique example of its kind.

The exceptionally rich museum, though free and very little visited, gives a better understanding of the origins of Japan's indigenous religious beliefs and practices. There are a phenomenal number of objects of all kinds, some dating back to prehistory.

The phallic aspect of certain objects relating to Tanokami (see box) might ruffle some prudish feathers, but the fertility and abundance of the harvest is a recurring theme in Shinto animism.

As well as the religious exhibits, the museum has an extensive collection of pottery and archaeological artefacts, and explores the spiritual origins of modern Japan.

Ta-no-kami: the protective spirit of the rice fields

Faithful to the Shinto principle where everything can be spirit, Ta-no-kami (田の神) is the deification of rice fields, the protective spirit of the harvest. The phallic aspect of some representations is linked to fertility and the crops that are obviously desired in abundance. The tradition is ancient: agricultural deities (Uka-no-mitama-no-kami, Toyo-uke-bime-no-kami and O-toshi-no-kami) were already mentioned in the *Kojiki* and *Nihon shoki*, the oldest official histories of Japan. Ta-no-kami is a popular deity, varying in form and substance, sometimes coming down from the mountains in spring. His appearance is often fluid. Stone statues on Kyushu island (south-west) depict him in human form and rather smiley. In the east of the country, Tanokami and *Ebisu* (god of fishermen) have become one, while in the west the same has happened with Tanokami and *Daikokuten*.

BUILDING NO. 1, AOYAMA TECHNICAL COLLEGE

The building that aspired to be a robot

7-9 Uguisudanicho, Shibuya-ku (東京都渋谷区鶯谷町 7-9)
10-minute walk from Shibuya station (渋谷), JR Yamanote, Saikyo or Shonan Shinjuku lines; Tokyu Toyoko or Den-en-Toshi lines; Keio Inokashira line; Tokyo metro Hanzomon, Ginza or Fukutoshin lines
Closed to the public, can be seen from outside

A few blocks from the busy Shibuya intersection, Aoyama Technical College (青山製図専門学校) is a private establishment training architects and interior designers that opened in the late 1970s.

The brainchild of architect Makoto Sei Watanabe[1] in 1990, Building No. 1 on the campus is an amazing achievement that stands out from its surroundings. It's a little over-the-top, with the air of a combat robot from science fiction. In what serves as a roof, reddish metal pipes seem to spring from the building, supported by cables connected to what could be taken for the head of the machine.

The interior is closed to the public.

NEARBY
Tokyo branch of Miki Corporation ⑱

Aoyama Technical College isn't the only architecturally striking achievement in and around Shibuya.

At 3-9-7 Shibuya, the offices of the Tokyo branch of Miki Corporation, a Kansai enterprise known for its plum-based products, were installed in March 1985 in a highly original building erected at an intersection. It was designed by Takenaka Corporation, which also built it. The first signs of the financial bubble were on the horizon at the time of construction, and it shows. The offices are in a building set back from the street that seems to have no windows on its main façade. The whole thing looks like a cross between an ancient pyramid and a tent in an Arabian desert.

[1] 渡辺誠. *1952–*.

DAIKANYAMA E-SUNFLOWER

Shopping under the petals of a solar flower

17-6 Daikanyamacho, Shibuya-ku (東京都渋谷区代官山町 17-6)
5-minute walk from Daikanyama station (代官山), Tokyu Toyoko line

At the heart of the chic shopping district of Daikanyama, opposite the post office, stands an amazing electronic sunflower (エレクトロニックひまわり), a good 10 metres high. The work of Polish artist Piotr Kowalski[1] in 2000, this decorative sunflower is covered with solar panels and its petals shine at night.

There are plenty more urban artworks in the area, but not the size of the sunflower. You can, for example, break up your shopping sessions by having a rest at the foot of a stack of elegant green peas. Each side of the steps at the back of Daikanyama Address, leading to the residential tower, is decorated with a series of coloured curved objects by Portuguese artist José de Guimarães.[2] On

the north side of the complex, a small plantation of (real) sunflowers can be found in the middle of the road.

Development of the Daikanyama Address complex where the sunflower stands, completed in 2000, really launched the modernization of the district.

The area has now become a more hip and elegant cousin of Shibuya, crowned with the opening in 2011 of the T-Site cultural centre at 17-5 Sarugakucho. With an impressive metal wolf on the garden side, T-Site also has its urban decorative art.

[1] 1927–2004.
[2] 1939–.

TOKYO MOSQUE

An Istanbul mosque in central Tokyo

1-19 Oyamacho, Shibuya-ku (東京都渋谷区大山町 1-19)
5 minutes from Yoyogi-Uehara station (代々木上原), Tokyo metro Chiyoda
or Odakyu lines
Admission free
Cultural centre open daily 10am–6pm
Mosque visit (including during prayers) for groups of less than five –
pre-booking required for larger groups
Free guided tours in Japanese, Saturday and Sunday at 2.30pm

slam, although a minority religion in Japan, is still present thanks to immigration from Asian countries with large Muslim populations, such as Indonesia and Malaysia. There are a dozen Muslim places of worship in Tokyo, but the most photogenic is undeniably Tokyo Camii (東京ジャーミイ), known as the Tokyo Mosque.

The mosque was founded by Tatars from Kazan[1] who fled the Russian Revolution via the trans-Siberian railway and Manchuria before reaching Japan in the 1920s. The group, led by Bashkir imam Muhammed-Gabdulkhay Kurbangaliev, founded a Muslim school for the children of the new immigrants in the late 1920s, which was moved here in 1935. The mosque was built next door and opened with great fanfare in 1938. The original building was demolished in 1986 and replaced in 2000 by a building constructed with the support of Turkey (Tatar refugees in Japan can obtain Turkish citizenship). The mosque also has a Turkish cultural centre. The very Ottoman style clashes sharply with the surrounding residential area. The interior is open to all, even during prayers, provided you're dressed respectably and women cover their hair with a scarf.

Shimokita and its forgotten past of Nazism, prostitution and rock'n'roll

Not far from the mosque, Shimokitazawa has a chequered and little-known history, where prostitution then rock'n'roll took over from Nazism. In 1941, a delegation of Hitler Youth visited the shopping area. In the late 60s the neighbourhood became a fellatio mecca with some rather specialized salons.

The district changed again in the 70s and started to rock, hosting clubs and punk concerts before, in the 2000s, becoming a merry circus of anything and everything, a hotbed of youth culture. A widely criticized urban planning project, finally adopted in 2006, envisages a different Shimokita – cleaner, more organized, wiser, perhaps easier to live in.

The railway operator Odakyu buried the tracks a few metres below ground and built another station underground in March 2013. A major road artery should pass just north of the station, dividing the neighbourhood. These rationalization plans for a neighbourhood where chaos is key have, unsurprisingly, met with strong opposition from artists, who prefer a looser organization. Shimokita risks losing its identity

[1] *In what is now Tatarstan, Russian Federation, where most of the inhabitants speak Tatar.*

Edogawa / Katsushika / Adachi

TONERI IKIIKI PARK

A little-known theme park inspired by Japanese folktales

6-3-1 Toneri, Adachi-ku (東京都足立舎人 6-3-1)
10-minute walk from Minumadai-Shinsuikoen station (見沼代親水公園),
Nippori-Toneri Liner
Open 24/7
Admission free

In the heart of an area only recently connected to the city centre by the Nippori-Toneri Liner, Toneri Ikiiki (舎人いきいき公園) is a children's park opened in the late 1990s. It isn't well known, so only local residents tend to go there.

The park has a series of outdoor games based on Japanese tales and legends, such as the fishing statue in the middle of the sandbox referencing *Momotaro*, or sea god Ryujin's castle that children can climb and explore. You'll find the turtle saved by fisher lad Urashima Taro and a seabream from the same legend.

The highlight of the park is perhaps an impressive red devil-shaped slide, giving the impression of spitting out any toddlers who have the courage to climb up inside it.

Toneri Ikiiki is far from being a crowd-puller, but its themes are original enough to make it almost a cultural outing for children.

HIGH-FREQUENCY TRANSMITTER ②
IN KITASHIKAHAMA PARK

Anti-hooligan device

3-26-1 Shikahama, Adachi-ku (東京都足立区鹿浜 3-26-1)
25-minute walk from Nishi-Araidaishi-Nishi station (西新井大師西),
Nippori-Toneri Liner; or 5 minutes from Sangyodoro-Higashi bus stop (産業道
路東); Kokusai Kogyo line 赤23 from Nishi-Araidashi-Nishi station
Accessible 24/7

Proving that the city takes its delinquency problems seriously, almost 2 kilometres west of the Nippori-Toneri Liner station, just north of the Kan-7 road, Kitashikahama Park (北鹿浜公園) had a high-frequency sound emitter rather like an anti-rat device installed in May 2009. The frequency range (around 17.6 kHz) is apparently inaudible to humans but unbearable for the hooligans, rogues and scoundrels (in other words, youths aged 10 to 20) who until then had hung about the park at night.

A month after the transmitter had been installed, however, the toilets were vandalized overnight. So in 2010 the local authorities abandoned that idea and posted a guard instead, but you can still see the device on the outside wall of the toilets. For the record, in 2009–2010 there was apparently a spike in the number of gangs wanting to check if they could hear the legendary frequency.

The park itself is a simple family affair, with a little train, a few bikes and pedal cars for hire, an old locomotive and some children's games. There's even a mini-pool for the summer.

Adachi facing up to delinquency

Since 2013, Adachi ward no longer holds the unfortunate tally of the highest number of reported crimes and misdemeanours – that prize now goes to Shinjuku. As cycle thefts represent about 30 per cent of the some 9,000 offences reported annually, the image of a lawless district plagued by delinquency and at the mercy of gangsters is somewhat exaggerated. Yet this is the burden that Adachi has borne for many years and is now trying to shake off, by all possible means.

IKO ARCHAEOLOGICAL PARK

*Economic hub of the Kanto region long ago...
very long ago*

4-9-1 Higashi-Iko, Adachi-ku (東京都足立区東伊興 4-9-1)
20-minute walk from Takenotsuka station (竹ノ塚), Tobu Skytree line;
or 5 minutes from Kita-Teramachi bus stop (北寺町); Tobu Central line 竹 04
from Takenotsuka • Open 10am–4pm, closed December 28 to January 4

The far north of Adachi offers a few sights for anybody curious enough to venture out there.

Iko Archaeological Park (伊興遺跡公園), for example, has a full-size replica of a prehistoric cave dwelling. In a corner of the park, inside a small and very well-organized free museum, are reproductions of life in the Jomon and Kofun periods and a few finds, mostly restored pieces of pottery from archaeological excavations at this obviously important site.

Unless you come across a local school trip, there's a good chance of finding yourself alone in this excellent museum, given the distance to the nearest station. You'll discover that Iko is one of the country's main (pre)historic sites up to the Kofun period, with masses of pottery and tumuli.

It's interesting to discover that the economic, spiritual and cultural heart of the entire region two millennia ago was, it seems, along the banks of the Kenagagawa and the former course of the Togegawa, well away from the towers of Marunouchi, Yaesu or Shinjuku.

NEARBY

Iko temple village   ④
A group of temples moved here after the 1923 earthquake

A few steps from the archaeological park, a series of a dozen or so temples known as Iko temple village (伊興寺町 – *Iko teramachi*) occupies an entire block at 4-Higashi-Iko. A minor curiosity of the district, yet completely ignored by the rest of the city and the country, the block in question looks almost Kyoto-like, except the temple construction is recent and concrete has appropriately supplanted the wooden structures. These temples were moved in the late 1920s after the Great Kanto Earthquake as part of the city reconstruction plan. The group is aesthetically pleasing, tranquil and photogenic enough to stroll around. You'll find the grave of Keishoin,[1] mother of Tsunayoshi,[2] the 5th Tokugawa shogun, and a statue of Hotei, one of the stages of the pilgrimage to Adachi's seven deities of good fortune.

---

[1] 桂昌院, *1627–1705. Concubine of the 3rd shogun, Tokugawa Iemitsu.*
[2] 徳川綱吉, *1646–1709, shogun from 1680 to his death. The initiator of some surprising laws, particularly the Shorui awaremi no rei series (*生類憐れみの令 *–Compassion Laws, literally "Edicts of Compassion towards Living Beings"), prohibiting the killing of animals, leading to a proliferation of stray dogs in Edo in the*

JIZOS OF NISHIARAI-DAISHI

Ward off warts and miscarriages

1-15-1 Nishiarai, Adachi-ku (東京都足立区西新井 1-15-1)
Daishi-Mae subway (大師前), Tobu line-Daishi
Open 6am–8pm daily

Not far from the main gate of the vast Zoji-ji, a shelter protects the temple's salt-covered statue of *Jizo*, apparently effective against warts. You take a little of *Jizo*'s salt when praying and rub it on your wart, and when it disappears offer the statue twice the amount of salt you used.

Farther along is another gleaming statue of *Jizo*. Much less familiar than its counterpart in Sugamo, this *Jizo* has to be sprinkled with water (延命水洗い地蔵) and is best known for granting longevity.

Another important Jizo of the temple, a sombre *Jizo Mizuko* (水子地蔵), is dedicated to miscarried, aborted or stillborn children, and any others who never had the chance to know their parents.

Zoji-ji: the only temple in Tokyo for "protection against evil"

Zoji-ji, aka Nishiarai-Daishi (西新井大師), is rich in history and tradition. In spiritual terms this is one of the most important temples to the north of the city and one of the Shingon sect's "Big Three Kanto temples for protection against evil" (関東厄除三大師) and the only one in Tokyo. The main building was reconstructed in 1972 after a devastating fire in 1966 but the main door is authentic and dates from the late Edo period.

NEARBY

Tobu-Daishi line ⑥

Two stops over a kilometre

Tobu-Daishi railway line, opened in 1931, is a curious track of just over a kilometre with only two stops. Serving Zoji-ji from Daishi-Mae stop (大師前), the line is a relic of an early 20th century plan to connect Nishiarai to Itabashi. The 1923 earthquake, excavations of the Arakawa, the economic crisis and war all disrupted its planning and construction, leaving only tiny metallic inroads over a distance that could easily be covered on foot. The line was even shortened to make way for the Kan-7 road before the project was finally abandoned in 1964, although some people still dream of a north Tokyo with rail links to Itabashi and beyond. Considering the limited number of trains, it's nearly always quicker to walk between Nishiarai and Daishi-Mae. Note there are no ticket machines at Daishi-Mae and the station is normally unstaffed: no ticket inspectors, no guards.

REMAINS OF SENJU *SHUKUBA* ⑦

The grandest entrance to the city

Around 3-33 Senju, Adachi-ku (東京都足立区千住 3-33)
5 minutes from Kita-Senju station (北千住), JR Joban line; Tokyo metro
Chiyoda or Hibiya lines; Isezaki (Tobu Skytree Line), MIR Tsukuba express

Senju *shukuba* (千住宿場), historically the first and largest of the four main *shukubas* on the way out of Edo (see p. 155), extended approximately 3 kilometres from the north of the Senju-Ohashi Bridge along the road to Mito and Nikko. The *honjin* that used to be at 3-33 Senju is today marked by a simple stone. A plaque in the nearby alley also gives a short history.

The historic route has become a narrow, busy shopping street, Shukubamachi-dori. Most of the *shukuba* has disappeared but the area is still dotted with a mass of temples and a few shrines, as well as some very old buildings. It's easy to spend the day wandering around in search of the many hidden relics of the golden age of this neighbourhood that is often completely overlooked by tourists.

Machi no Eki, a miniscule free information centre that details the multiple hidden traces of the *shukuba*, has been installed in a restored fishmonger's at 3-69 Senju. There you can get maps of the various historic sites still standing. At 4-28-1, for example, you'll discover a superb building that used to belong to an Edo paper merchant, still in excellent condition (it's privately occupied, so closed to the public). Other historic homes can be seen at 5-19-11 and 5-6-7. At 5-22-1, the Nagura clinic is open on the site of a *honetsugi* (bone setter) dating from the 18th century.

To understand the *shukuba* better, on the 10th floor of the Marui department store at the station, just opposite the elevator exit, is a very impressive model of part of the station on a scale of 1/50.

When the *shukuba* was gone, Kita-Senju remained an important transport hub with the arrival of the railway, unlike Itabashi-shuku (see p. 154) and Shinagawa-shuku (p. 61).

BRONZE STATUES OF *KOCHIKAME* CHARACTERS

Keeping the peace in Kameari Park

Around 36-5 Kameari, Katsushika-ku (東京都葛飾区亀有 36-5)
Kameari station (亀有), JR Joban line
Accessible 24/7

Representing the fiery, blundering police officer and his colleagues who keep the peace in the neighbourhood, fourteen statues of characters from the *Kochikame* manga stand around near Kameari station (亀有), five to the north (including the main character Ryotsu Kankichi, aka Ryo-san) and nine to the south.

Kochikame, in full *Kochira Katsushikaku Kameari Koenmae Hashutsujo* (こちら葛飾区亀有公園前派出所 – This is the Police Box in front of Kameari Park in Katsushika Ward), is now the best-selling manga ever. It first appeared in issue 42 of *Weekly Shonen Jump* in September 1976 and is still published weekly.

Disappointingly for fans, there's no police box in front of Kameari Park, 50 metres north of the station. The nearest one is at the north exit of the station.

The famous park could almost be anywhere, with its sandbox, swings and wooden castle: a local park like so many others. But happily a bronze Ryo is sitting on one of the benches, probably checking that all's well, and another Ryo gaily poses for a photo.

Placement of the statues

Character	Location
Ryotsu Kankichi 両津勘吉	Station concourse, north side
Reiko Catherine Akimoto 秋本・カトリーヌ・麗子	Near police box, north exit of station
Ryotsu Kankichi 両津勘吉	Junction of Kameari Ketsueki Centre Mae and 5-14 Kameari
Ryotsu Kankichi 両津勘吉	In Kameari Park 36-5 Kameari
Ryotsu Kankichi 両津勘吉	On a bench in Kameari Park 36-5 Kameari
Ryotsu Kankichi 両津勘吉	In front of the toilets on the station concourse, south exit
Ryotsu Kankichi 両津勘吉	On a bench at a bus stop at the station's south exit
Nakagawa Keiichi 中川圭一	In front of Lilio 2 shopping centre 3-29 Kameari
Akimoto Catherine Reiko 秋本・カトリーヌ・麗子	Between Lilio and the railway track, south exit of station, 3-26 Kameari
Ryotsu Kankichi 両津勘吉	In front of Truth building 3-18-4 Kameari
Three children, Ton, Chin, Kan トン・チン・カン (Kankichi bambino)	In front of building 3-15-8 Kameari
Honda Hayato 本田速人	Along Route 467 3-13-1 Kameari
Ryotsu Kankichi 両津勘吉	Along Route 467 2-63-7 Kameari
Ryotsu Kankichi 両津勘吉	Precincts of Katori-Jinja shrine 3-42 Kameari

JIZO STATUE ALL TRUSSED UP ⑨

String along to keep your partner or to ward off burglars

Nanzoin temple
2-28-5 Higashi-Mizumoto, Katsushika-ku (東京都葛飾区東水元 2-28-5)
15 minutes from Kanamachi station (金町), JR Joban line; 3 minutes from
Shibarare-jizo bus stop (しばられ地 蔵); Keisei line 金 61 from Kanamachi
Open 9am–4pm daily

In Narihirasan Nanzoin temple (業平山南蔵院), not far from Mizu-moto Park, a curious stone statue of *Jizo* stands 1 metre high.

As he's completely trussed up in several layers of string, his face is sometimes hidden. This *Jizo* dates from the early 18th century, and the tradition is to attach a string to request a wish, then loosen it once the wish has been granted.

Obviously, *Jizo* is believed to grant wishes where "attachment" is important: against theft, to hang onto someone and prevent them from leaving, etc.

Pieces of string are available in return for a small donation on the right side of the statue.

In addition to *Jizo*, you'll find an authentic *suikinkutsu* at the rear of the pleasant and very well-maintained temple gardens.

Nanzoin, originally sited near the Skytree tower, suffered significant damage in the 1923 earthquake. *Jizo* and the temple had to be moved here.

Jizo: a major police inquiry of the Edo period

The trussed-up Jizo was at the heart of a major police affair in the early 18th century.

The story goes that a cloth merchant slumbering on a summer's day in the grounds of the Jizo temple had his produce stolen while he slept. Edo magistrate Oooka Tadasuke, investigating the case (see p. 43), ordered Jizo's arrest as he'd failed in his duty to watch over the temple enclosure.

Curious onlookers gathered in the administrative offices and the magistrate, changing his tone, imposed a fine on them all, payable in cloth, for entering the enclosure without permission. When he and the merchant compared the pieces of cloth they were given, the magistrate was able to break up the ring of thieves. Jizo was released and thanks were given for his help with the investigation.

Koaidame, a territorial dispute between Saitama and Tokyo?

Scarcely 200 metres north of Nanzoin, the Koaidame reservoir in Mizumoto Park (Tokyo's largest park, as so often forgotten) was the origin of a minor dispute between Saitama and Tokyo.

According to Katsushika ward, as the reservoir forms part of the park, the border with the town of Misato in Saitama prefecture is therefore on the Misato bank of the river and the reservoir as a whole is in Tokyo.

For Misato, the reservoir (even if artificial) should be treated like a river, and the border between Tokyo and Saitama is in the middle of Koaidame.

To date, no important oil field has been found under the reservoir, and the fish stocks probably consist of some river and shellfish that don't demand high-level negotiations, so the dispute probably won't escalate. At the eastern end of the park and reservoir, you'll find a fun permanent exhibition of goldfish promoted by Katsushika: the collection has around a thousand multicoloured fish of various species in about forty outdoor basins.

The border between Saitama and Tokyo passes through the exhibition and technically only some of the basins are in Tokyo (on that, everyone agrees).

PARK ON THE BANKS OF THE HIKIFUNEGAWA

Walk along a former Edo canal

4-1 Hikifunegawa, Katsushika-ku (東京都葛飾区亀有 4-1)
10-minute walk from Yotsugi station (四ツ木), Keisei Oshiage line
Accessible 24/7

About 800 metres north-west of Yotsugi along Route 6, the green corridor with a little stream running through it (*Hikifunegawa*, 曳 舟川 – River of Towed Boats) is all that's left of a canal dating from the Edo period.

The canal was used as a transport route in the late Edo and early Meiji by boats towed along from the banks by men or beasts, hence its name. Although the canal was much longer, the corridor now stretches a good 3 kilometres, almost as far as Kameari. Its entire length is now a municipal park, appropriately named the Park on the Banks of the Hikifunegawa (曳舟川親水公園). But this isn't the original watercourse, as the canal was filled in long ago.

The park has a number of modest attractions and noticeboards with historical descriptions.

The stream is only a few centimetres deep, just enough for kids to take a dip in summer at the three sites provided, without worrying their parents overmu.

NEARBY

Katsushika City Museum ⑪

The official English translation, Katsushika City Museum (葛飾区郷 土と天文の博物館), located alongside the park at 3-25-1 Shiratori, doesn't do justice to the poetic tone of the original Japanese name. Rather than just a history museum, this is a "local history and astronomy museum" – local but eclectic, including both a planetarium and a collection of historical objects, such as prehistoric statuettes from the district. The museum is a catch-all in the best sense: from exhibitions on the Mars Explorer to a Foucault pendulum, a solar telescope, a depiction of Katsushika when it was an agricultural area, and life in the neighbourhood in the 1950s…

STATUES OF CAPTAIN TSUBASA

Soccer manga still in good shape

1-22-3 Yotsugi, Katsushika-ku (東京都葛飾区四つ木 1-22-3)
Yotsugi station (四ツ木), Keisei Oshiage line
Accessible 24/7

Yotsugi Tsubasa-koen is a new green sward in the city, revamped in late March 2013, to the west of Yotsugi station at 1-22-3 Yotsugi. The park is known for its bronze statue of Ozora Tsubasa, the soccer anime and manga character (*Captain Tsubasa*, キャプテン翼), for anyone who doesn't already know or might have forgotten.

Author Takahashi Yoichi[1] is from this rarely visited part of town, which needed a crowd-puller. This statue of Tsubasa isn't the only one: seven different cartoon characters are dotted around between Yotsugi and Tateishi, sometimes directly on the roadside like the small statue of Nakazawa Sanae, and sometimes farther away, as in Shibue Park just over the Keisei railway, where Misaki Taro stands.e Tateishi, talvolta direttamente lungo la strada, come per esempio nel Parco di Shibue, subito dopo aver attraversato le rotaie della Keisei, dove svetta una statua di Misaki Taro (Ben Becker).

The statues

Characters (Japanese)	Characters (European)	Location
Ozora Tsubasa (大空翼)	Olivier "Holly" Atton	Yotsugi Tsubasa Park 1-22-3 Yotsugi
Ishizaki Ryo (石崎了)	Bruce Harper	On a level with the railway track near municipal service point 1-15-1 Yotsugi
Hyuga Kojiro (日向小次郎)	Mark Landers	Yotsugi Tsubasa Park 1-16-24 Yotsugi
Roberto Hongo (ロベルト本 with Ozora Tsubasa	Roberto Sedinho	Near staircase leading to footbridge 2-3-3 Yotsugi
Nakazawa Sanae (中沢早苗)	Patty Gatsby	Front of post office 2-28-1 Yotsugi
Misaki Taro (岬太郎)	Ben Becker	Shibue Park 3-3-1 Higashi Tateishi
Wakabayashi Genzo (若林 源三)	Benjamin "Benji" Price	Along the street 4-28-14 Tateishi
Ozora Tsubasa (大空翼)	Olivier Atton	Tateishi children's park 1-21-6 Tateishi

¹ 高橋陽一, 1960–.

STATUE AT CHIKUSA CELLULOID FACTORY

Kewpie dolls made here

3-3-1 Higashi-Tateishi, Katsushika-ku (東京都葛飾区東立石 3-3-1)
10-minute walk from Tateishi station (京成立石), Keisei Honsen line
Accessible 24/7

A rather unexpected statue of three dolls in one corner of Shibue Park is a reminder that this is the site of a former toy manufacturer: Chikusa celluloid factory (千種セルロイド工業).

The factory, opened in 1914, marked the launch of the Katsushika celluloid industry, which had supported the district's industrial development before the war.

It mass-produced the legendary Kewpie dolls before celluloid was banned in the 1950s because of its high flammability, an inexcusable and very embarrassing defect for a material used in children's toys.

The two Kewpies aren't the same ...

In the Japanese collective consciousness, the chubby baby designed by American writer and illustrator Rose O'Neill in 1909 was closely associated with the mayonnaise manufacturer Kewpie Corporation, which used the character as its logo. Kewpie Corporation was however established ten years after the baby doll, and only started to produce mayonnaise in 1925. Taking advantage of the little character, the manufacturers initially used a popular name and tweaked it a bit. The doll is called Kewpie, *Kyupi* (キューピー) in Japanese; the product name is pronounced in the same way but transliterated as *Kiyupi* (キユーピー), officially a "graphic choice". To complicate matters, until 2010 the Kewpie Corporation was written Q.P. in English, before taking the current spelling. Anyway, the two Kewpies aren't the same ...

NEARBY
Shibue playground ⑭
Superwide slide

Shibue Park, opened on the site after the factory closed, is a den of delights for local families, especially the residents of two imposing twenty-storey municipal tower blocks, Yotsugi 4-chome, just opposite the park. Shibue also has an attractive flower meadow (very photogenic in season), tennis courts, and a variety of children's play equipment, including a wonderfully wide slide (dating from the 1960s) which several children can use at the same time. With the statue of the popular soccer manga Taro Misaki (see p. 205), the Chikusa factory memorial and this slide, Shibue is an almost ideal place for a quirky family outing.

STANDING STONE OF TATEISHI

⑮

Sacred stone in a residential area

8-37-17 Tateishi, Sumida-ku (東京葛飾区立石 8-37-17)
10 minutes from Tateishi station (京成立石), Keisei Honsen line
Accessible 24/7

Protected by a *torii* hidden away in a children's park at 8-37-17 Tateishi, the *Tateishisama* (立石様 – Standing Stone), which gave its name to the district, is in the middle of a group of apartment buildings.

The stone, probably the remains of a mound once used as a route marker, barely rises from the surface although it was easy to spot in the Edo era. Subsidence in the east of the city, and then, it seems, the superstitious who came to chip off a piece of stone for protection during the wars with Russia and China, reduced the stone to what it is today: an ambiguous piece of rock set in sandy soil, yet protected with the utmost care. If you weren't aware of its origins, the small enclosure round this corner of the park might seem rather mysterious.

NEARBY
Tateishi Nakamise ⑯
1960s arcade

Just across from Tateishi station, on the south side, two covered arcades stand out from the city's traditional shopping streets. Although the first (Tateishi Eki Dori – 立石駅通り　商店街) is interesting, it's the second, Tateishi Nakamise (立石仲見世), that really deserves attention. Nakamise, set up in 1945 in the chaos of post-war reconstruction, simply pressed the "pause" button in the 1960s. Although it's not the longest or (by far) the most popular, it's one of the city's most surprising covered arcades, with its series of greasy-spoon cafés and other joints in a world that seems almost out of the history books, taking into account the postwar doldrums and the beginning of Japan's economic miracle. Above a storefront at its southern end, some black and white photographs evoke the neighbourhood story of late industrialization and celluloid factories (see p. 207). It's a magical place for those who appreciate that sort of thing. The retro atmosphere also overflows onto the streets farther south of Okudo Kaido (奥戸街道), behind the arcade. Several other stalls add to the ambience until the city gradually plunges into residential torpor as you leave the station behind.

SHOGAN-JI PLANETARIUM

Dwarfs, whale and dinosaur

7-11-30 Tateishi, Katsushika-ku (東京都葛飾区立石 7-11-30)
5-minute walk from Tateishi station (京成立石), Keisei Oshiage line;
or 8 minutes from Aoto station (青砥), Keisei Honsen line
Open daily 8.30am–4.30pm
Projections first and third Saturdays of the month at 3pm
Reservations at www.gingaza.jp

Help a local family in need at smud.org/EnergyHELP

1

Choose an amount

You determine the amount you can give each month.

2

Select a charity

Your donation is made to a trusted partner.

3

Help your community

The charity partner connects with a neighbor in need and pays their electric bill.

4

Feel good

Thanks for helping keep the lights on! You'll see your donation on your SMUD bill.

SMUD®

Help a local family in need keep the lights on for as little as $5.

Scan this QR code or visit
smud.org/EnergyHELP

SMUD®

At 7-11-30 Tateishi, in the centre of the new Shitamachi, not far from the spectacular Katsushika Symphony Hills cultural venue with its statues to the glory of classical music, in 1996 Shogan-ji opened a small but authentic planetarium known as Gingaza (銀河座). On the first and third Saturdays of the month at 3pm, the temple organizes a projection for twenty-five lucky people, accompanied by explanations in an almost comical style (in Japanese). Book online to see the show.

The temple precincts also have their eccentric touches, including the head priest, Kasuga Ryo (春日了).[1]

The two statuettes of dwarfs bleached by the years, standing beside the lion statue guarding the temple, are straight out of Disney and take you aback. A surprising statue of a Chasmosaurus (a species of dinosaur like the Triceratops) on the other side of the main building twins the guardian lion. Finally, note the huge spaceship on the wall of the planetarium building and the whale mural, neither of them very subtle.

[1] 春日了

GIANT DAMS ON THE EDOGAWA ⑱

Bulwarks against the waters

6-22-19 Shibamata, Katsushika-ku (東京都葛飾区柴又 6-22-19)
15 minutes from Shibamata station (柴又), Keisei Kanamachi line

Tokyo's overflowing rivers can cause considerable damage over a vast and very low-lying area that has been particularly densely populated for a century. Although the 1917 flood "only" killed 260 people, the risk today is much greater.

To counteract the vagaries of the river, the Edogawa is surmounted by giant dams protecting Tokyo (and Chiba prefecture). They're so big that paradoxically it's sometimes difficult to spot them.

High up in Shibamata Park (柴又公園), next to the famous Taisha-kuten temple, is a good place from which to take in the scale of the structures. This 1-hectare park, opened in 1997, covers one of the finished dams. There is also an explanatory plan of the super-dams (スーパー堤防), colossal structures some 10 metres high and 200–300 metres wide.

The structure of the dam encloses the Tora-san Museum (葛飾柴又 寅さん記念館), dedicated to Kuruma Torajiro (車寅次郎) from Shibamata, hero of the prolific film series *Otoko ha tsurai yo* (男はつらい よ – It's Hard to Be a Man).

Tokyo, a city reclaimed from the water

Tokyo's history since the Edo period has been punctuated by its continuing extension into the bay. The castle that Tokugawa Ieyasu took over in the late 16th century and which became the Imperial Palace, does indeed face the wide mouth of the Hirakawa, Hibiya Irie (日比谷入江). Opposite the castle, on the other side of the river, roughly at the level of modern Tokyo station, stretched the Edomaeshima sandbar. Farther east lay a succession of ponds and swamps. The shores of the bay were scarcely farther to the south than the modern Sobu line. The shogunate swiftly launched the colossal task of drying out or diverting the watercourses to make way for the burgeoning city with its population explosion. Tsukiji (築地 – "built land") was founded in 1658, and many of the iconic Chuo neighbourhoods were built on reclaimed land or made habitable in the 17th century. Beyond the Sumida River, the city gradually advanced towards the south, criss-crossed with canals (Onagigawa top of the list) for the passage of cargo boats.

Construction sites were everywhere throughout the Meiji and Taisho eras and in the early Showa. In the south, the city stretched serenely eastwards. The Shiomi neighbourhood rose from the waters of the bay during the 20th century, before the outbreak of war, and the city reached Toyosu. After the war the pace accelerated and Odaiba expanded in the 1960s and 70s. Work on the Rainbow Bridge began in 1987 and ended in 1993.

Behind the Gate Bridge and extending farther into the water, Chuo-Bohatei landfill (see p. 296) is the latest bite taken out of Tokyo Bay.

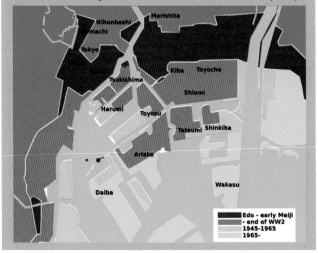

TOWER HALL FUNABORI OBSERVATORY

An unusual view of the eastern plains

4-1-1 Funabori, Edogawa-ku (東京都江戸川区船堀 4-1-1)
Funabori station (船堀), Toei subway Shinjuku line
Observatory open 9am–9.30pm

Tower Hall Funabori (タワーホール船堀), just north of Funabori station, is a municipal building opened in 1999 and topped with a 115-metre tower.

The complex includes several function rooms and cinemas but, most interestingly, an observatory at the top of the tower. Entry is free and offers a clear 360-degree view as there are very few high buildings in the vicinity. The district's only taller structure is the giant 117-metre Diamond and Flower Ferris Wheel, which you can see to the south in Kasai Rinkai Park. The view to the west is over the urban sprawl of the city centre against a backdrop of Mount Fuji, weather permitting, with the imposing presence of the Arakawa and Tokyo Skytree tower a little closer. The observatory's late opening hours mean that you can get a superb and little-known evening view of the city, from a very unusual angle.

NEARBY
Zenshinsha ⑳
Revolutionary stronghold

A little east of Route 308, in the heart of the straight residential streets of Edogawa, about 20 minutes' walk north of Funabori, you'll see a strange building: protected by a thick layer of green metal sheets at 1-12-7 Matsue, it is officially the seat of Zenshinsha publishing house (前進社). In fact, it's the headquarters of the national committee of the Revolutionary Communist League (革命的共産主義者同盟全国委員会), nicknamed *Chukaku-ha* (中核派 – Central Faction).

Founded in the 1950s, *Chukaku-ha* is a group of far-left, anti-capitalist, anti-Stalinist anti-imperialists who advocate revolution through violence. Still rooted in some university campuses, and active despite the numerous regular arrests of its members, it has claimed responsibility for several arson and bomb attacks (sometimes deadly), especially in the 1970s and 80s. It has on record a few spectacular strikes, such as the rocket attack on the Geihinkan at the Tokyo summit of 1986. Getting on for a hundred activists live full-time in this small stronghold, a fortified castle of modern times and target of regular police raids.

GATES OF THE OLD LOCK OF KOMATSUGAWA

㉑

When water courses sink

9-9 Oshima, Edogawa-ku (江戸川区大島 9-9)
10 minutes from Higashi-Ojima station (東大島), Toei subway Shinjuku line
Accessible 24/7

In Komatsugawa Park, a structure very similar to the battlements of a minor medieval fortress lies half buried. This curious building is actually the top of one of the doors of the old Komatsugawa lock (小松川閘門).

Built in 1930, it joined the Nakagawa and Arakawa until the 1970s. The two rivers were not actually at the same level, particularly following the subsidence of the city (see p. 281).

The difference in level between the two rivers has now reached 3 metres, and the Arakawa lock gate (荒川ロックゲート), completed in 2005 just south of Komatsugawa Park, allows for navigation between old Nakagawa and Arakawa.

You can climb into the very structure of the Arakawa lock gate via a short flight of steps, leading to a small observatory over the Arakawa. A panel below explains the importance of building the canal.

NEARBY

Nakagawa Funabansho Museum ㉒
Edo canals

The Nakagawa Funabansho Museum at 9-1-15 Oshima, dedicated to traffic on the canals and rivers of Edo and to local fishing history, is located 50 metres from a former barge/ship guard station (船番所 – *Funabansho*) of the Edo period, which itself stood at the ancient confluence of the Onagigawa, Nakagawa and Funaborigawa.

The museum is small and very specialized, but well organized. The second floor concentrates on the history of the district.

The very unusual "heart" of the exhibition is on the third floor, where visitors "walk on water" next to a transport barge docked on a reproduction of a guard station. The museum also has a fine collection of fishing gear.

Former bed of the Nakagawa

The few streams meandering around that make up the Kyu-Nakagawa (旧中川 – Old Naka River) are the only remains of the historical course of a mighty river disturbed by the widening in the last century of the Arakawa, which bisected it. These sections of riverbed are traces of the notoriously capricious Tonegawa, gradually diverted from Tokyo Bay to the Pacific by the work begun in the late 16th century.

Bunkyo / Toshima

WESTERN GRAVES AT SOMEI CEMETERY

A little-known witness to the first years of Japan's opening up to the world

A little-known witness to the first years of Japan's opening up to the world
5-5-1 Komagome, Toshima-ku (東京都豊島区駒込 5-5-1)
10-minute walk from Sugamo station (巣鴨), Toei subway Mita line or JR Yamanote line • Open 24/7

Somei cemetery (染 井 霊 園), just behind Toshima wholesale market, is the smallest of the cemeteries run by Tokyo Metropolitan Government. This secular cemetery, opened in 1874, is slightly less well-populated with historical celebrities than Zoshigaya and Yanaka cemeteries and is best known for the pink spring blossom of a hundred Somei-Yoshino cherry trees.

A tiny section of the cemetery (shown on the plans as 外人墓地 – *Gaijin-Bochi*) is given over to foreigners. The few graves with epitaphs in Roman script contrast sharply with the other rows. These graves dating back to the Meiji period belong to the first Western visitors to die in their host country. As these deaths were not high-profile, this section of the cemetery is a little-known testament to the early years of the country's opening up to the rest of the world and a memorial to those who lived through it.

You'll find, for example, the graves of Archibald King from Glasgow, who died of cholera in 1886; Reverend Woodhull, who died in Tokyo in 1895 aged 35; and missionary David Thompson, who had worked with James Hepburn[1] and died in 1915. Of particular note is the tomb of Loduska Wirick, a missionary nurse who arrived in Japan in 1890 and worked throughout the Russo-Japanese War. She died of cancer in 1914. Her prominent tombstone, in the form of a book, is clearly indicated by a white signpost.

Tomb of the Kingdom of Hawaii's Minister to Japan

Aoyama cemetery (青山霊園) is more centrally located and larger than Somei, and also busier. Its section for foreigners dates back to the Meiji period. The first burial, that of the German Karl Bruck, took place in 1880, three years after the government announced the opening of the cemetery to non-Japanese. A 2007 monument commemorates the contributions of foreigners who died working for the country's development. A notable tomb in the general section of the cemetery is that of Robert Walker Irwin, the Kingdom of Hawaii's Resident Minister in Japan, before Hawaii became part of the United States.

[1] *Inventor of the Hepburn method of romanizing Japanese.*

SUGAMO PRISON MARKER STONE

The dark past of Ikebukuro

3-1-6 Higashi-Ikebukuro, Toshima-ku (豊島区東池袋 3-1-6)
10-minute walk from Ikebukuro (池袋), JR Yamanote, Saikyo, Shonan-Shinjuku, Narita express, Tobu Tojo or Seibu Ikebukuro lines; Tokyo metro Yurakucho, Marunouchi or Fukutoshin lines

The 240-metre skyscraper Sunshine 60 of Sunshine City, at the time of building the highest in Asia, has since 1978 occupied the site of the infamous Sugamo prison (巣鴨拘置所), which mainly held political prisoners during the war, then war criminals after 1945.

The prison, administratively Tokyo's penitentiary before the Allied Occupation, has since been demolished, although it was spared the bombings. Seven Class A war criminals (guilty of crimes against peace), including Tojo Hideki,[1] were hanged there on 23 December 1948. Around fifty Class B (war crimes) and C (crimes against humanity) prisoners were also condemned to death.

Practically nothing is left of the prison and its dark past, except a simple stone, a monument to peace soberly entitled *Eikyu heiwa wo negatte* (永久平和を願って – Prayer for Eternal Peace).

It stands in Higashi Ikebukuro Chuo Park at the foot of Sunshine 60, a modest reminder of the history of the site. This monument stands where the former gallows were situated.

NEARBY

Labyrinth of 6-Otsuka and 5-Higashi Ikebukuro ③
An urban maze

Sandwiched between Route 5 of the urban expressway, Kasuga-dori and the Arakawa tramline lies a labyrinth of alleys, miraculous survivors of real-estate development and urban regeneration plans. Tokyo is full of narrow streets, but here they're particularly concentrated. Don't be afraid to go down what appears at first to be a dead end – some alleys are so narrow that they're difficult to negotiate on a bike, even if there are no steps. It's no surprise that the district has been designated a high-risk area for disaster management.

---

[1] 東条英機, *1884–1948. Prime minister of Japan 1941–1944.*

LOURDES

Reproduction of the miraculous French grotto in Tokyo

3-15-16 Sekiguchi, Bunkyo-ku (東京都文京区関 3-15-16)
10-minute walk from Edogawabashi station (江戸川橋), Tokyo metro
Yurakucho line
Accessible 24/7

At the end of the esplanade of St Mary's Cathedral, seat of the Roman Catholic Archdiocese of Tokyo, a discreet grotto contains a statue of the Virgin Mary. This is a reproduction of the grotto of Massabielle at Lourdes (ルルド) in France, where Bernadette Soubirous claimed to have had a vision of the Virgin on eighteen occasions during the year 1858, and where, on Mary's instructions, she is thought to have discovered the now famous miraculous source. Henri Demangelle, a French missionary in the Meiji era from Doubs in France, created this faithful reproduction in 1911. A monumental stone records the date of Bernadette's first vision in the Pyrenees – 11 February 1858.

Other Japanese replicas of the Lourdes grotto

This is the only grotto dedicated to the Virgin in Tokyo, but there are at least four others in the country – in Shizuoka, Nagoya, Nagasaki and the Goto Islands – erected in the late 19th and early 20th centuries.

Designed in 1964 by Tange Kenzo[1] (whose funeral was held here), St Mary's Cathedral, Tokyo (東京カテドラル聖マリア大聖堂), often referred to as Tokyo Cathedral, is a magnificent modern creation that replaced the old wooden Gothic building destroyed during the war. The cruciform building consists of eight hyperbolic paraboloids (curved saddle shapes) in reinforced concrete. Access is free and the interior, bare but for the play of light over its surfaces, is just as successful as the exterior. The reflections and contrasts against the blue sky are best appreciated on a sunny day. Photos not allowed, unfortunately. The small baptistery on the right as you enter is quite remarkable. At weekends, families queue to hold their wedding ceremonies at St Mary's.

[1] 丹下健三, 1913-2005. one of the leading Japanese architects of the 20th century, responsible for some outstanding designs ranging from Yoyogi Park's National Gymnasium to the Metropolitan Government buildings.

CHINZANSO ESTATE

Superb gardens of a grand hotel

2-10-8 Sekiguchi, Bunkyo-ku (東京都文京区関 2-10-8)
10-minute walk from Edogawabashi station (江戸川橋), Tokyo metro
Yurakucho line
Open 24/7

The lush gardens of the elegant Hotel Chinzanso Tokyo (椿山荘), formerly the Four Seasons, a 10-minute walk from Edogawabashi station, are open to the general public as well as hotel guests. The grounds formed part of the domain of the Maeda clan of Kururi in the Edo period.

The site at the edge of a plateau was called *Tsubaki-Yama* (椿山 – Mount of the Camellias), because of the flowers that grew there. When Meiji politician Yamagata Aritomo[1] acquired it in 1878 after crushing the Satsuma rebellion, he created sophisticated gardens that naturally became known as *Chinzanso* (椿山荘 – Domain of the Mount of the Camellias). In 1918, the estate came under the control of Baron Fujita Heitaro.[2] He brought a small shrine from Kyoto in 1924 to install in the garden and, in 1925, a three-storey pagoda dating from the Muromachi period, from Hiroshima prefecture.

Although the gardens suffered some damage during the Tokyo bombing, they have been beautifully restored and even enhanced. Several tearooms and rest points in the southern section were built after the war. The grounds, far from being flat, surround the large pond of Yusui-Ike. Particularly notable among the many points of interest are some twenty curious black *rakan* (Buddhist disciple) statuettes and a pretty thirteen-storey stone pagoda.

NEARBY
Basho residence

⑥

Behind Chinzanso at 2-11-3 Sekiguchi, along an alley up a flight of steps, a concealed entrance leads to Sekiguchi Basho-an (関口芭蕉庵). This was supposedly the home of the supreme Japanese haiku poet Matsuo Basho[3] during the four years he spent in Edo overseeing the renovation of Kanda aqueduct (see p. 233) in the late 17th century. Besides the tiny residence itself (an appealing post-war reproduction), a path leads around a pond where you'll find a stone inscribed with the poet's famous frog haiku, *Furu ike ya kawazu tobikomu mizu no oto* (古池や蛙飛びこむ 水の音 – The old pond, a frog jumps in, the sound of the water), based on his calligraphic writings. Another stele dating from 1750 marks the place where one of the master's poems is buried. At the far end of the garden, a small building was erected in 1726 to protect a wooden statue of Basho marking the thirty-second anniversary of his death. Admission to this simple, relaxing site is free.

[1] 山縣有朋, *1838–1922. Samurai of the Hagi domain, soldier and politician of the Meiji era, was one of the most powerful men of his time, holding successive ministerial posts and even becoming prime minister twice.*
[2] 藤田平太郎, *1869–1940. Businessman and politician, leader of the second Fujita zaibatsu.*
[3] 松尾芭蕉, *1644–1694. Classical poet, recognized master of haiku.*

BOTANICAL GARDENS AT TOKYO ⑦ UNIVERSITY'S GRADUATE SCHOOL OF SCIENCE

Gardens for everyone

3-7-1 Hakusan, Bunkyo-ku (東京都文京区白山 3-7-1)
15-minute walk from Hakusan station (白山), Toei subway Mita line
Open 9am–4.30pm every day except Monday – if Monday is a public holiday, the park is open, but closed the following day

Koishikawa Botanical Gardens of the University of Tokyo's Graduate School of Science (東京大学大学院理学系研究科附属植物園小石川植物園) are much less touristic than the nearby Koishikawa-Korakuen garden (with which they are sometimes confused). The gardens are just far enough from the nearest subway stations to discourage visitors, despite being one of the most appealing of the city's green havens.

There's something for everyone: Western gardens, Japanese gardens, a tropical greenhouse, a semi-wild forest, all in just over 16 hectares. Ad-

mission is free, but it's a small price to pay for tranquillity in the heart of the metropolis. The site was originally the medicinal herb garden of the Tokugawa shogunate in the 17th century and was then extended under the 8th shogun. Kurosawa Akira's[1] 1965 film *Akahige* (赤ひげ – Red Beard) is set in the clinic built in the gardens in 1723.

NEARBY

Koishikawa Annex, University of Tokyo Museum ⑧
First building on Todai campus

In the north-west corner of the gardens, an extremely elegant building from the early Meiji era overlooks a pond in the Japanese garden: the Koishikawa Annex of Tokyo University Museum (東京大学総合研究博物館小石川分館), formerly the main building of the medical school. This is actually the oldest building in the university, dating from 1875. Admission is free and an interesting architectural exhibition opened in late 2013. The annex is directly accessible from the botanical gardens, but once you've left the gardens you can't go back in.

[1] 黒澤明, *1910-1998. Film director.*

BLIND ENMA STATUE
AT GENKAKU-JI

Look after your eyes and teeth

Genkaku-ji
2-23-14 Koishikawa, Bunkyo-ku (東京都文京区小石川 2-23-14)
5-minute walk from Kasuga station (春日), Toei subway Mita or Oedo lines;
or from Korakuen station (後楽園), Tokyo metro Namboku or Marunouchi
lines
Open 7am–5pm daily

Genkaku-ji (源覚寺), a temple sandwiched between buildings along Kasuga-dori, offers an agreeable mix of ancient traditions (very much alive) that traditionally help you stay healthy.

The temple is known as Konnyaku Enma (こんにゃく閻魔 – Enma at Konnyaku), the custom being to offer *konnyaku* ("devil's tongue" seaweed paste) to the temple's Enma statue to give thanks to the deity. The practice dates back to the Edo period, when an elderly person with failing eyes had their sight restored after praying to Enma and gave thanks with an offering of *konnyaku*. Enma was thought to have lent his eyes. Note that the statue is blind. The cypress-wood statue of about 1 metre dates from the Kamakura era and was restored in the 17th century. It is not placed immediately at the entrance to the protective enmado, but is clearly visible inside. You can't always get close to it. A photo of the statue just in front of the *enmado* indicates where the *konnyaku* offerings should be made. Near the temple cemetery, to the right of the *enmado*, a small cabin protects two headless *Jizo* statues from the weather and other hazards. Here you have to sprinkle salt on the statue at the part of the body that hurts after touching it with a wand.

Whereas the temple's Enma has particular success with eyes, the two *Jizos* cure many things, especially toothache. The amount of salt piling up on these two *Jizos* can become really impressive. A standing stone at the entrance to the temple enclosure, worn at the base and topped with a little roof, is a *Hyakudo-ishi* (百度石 – Hundred Times Stone). This stone, erected in 1852, marks the starting point for believers who wish to make a pilgrimage of a hundred round trips (百度参り – Hundred Times Pilgrimage) in the precincts of the temple itself to multiply the effects of prayer. There are still some pebbles (but probably less than 100) placed in front of the stone, as the pilgrims place one pebble each time they pass to count the number of trips made.

Itinerary of a bell

The temple bell, cast in 1690, has had an eventful life. It was stored in 1844 after a fire, then in 1937 was sent to a temple in Saipan (then Japanese territory). Hit by a bullet, it went missing in 1944 in the chaos following the fall of the island to US-led Allies, probably taken home by a marine as a souvenir. It was found in 1965 in Texas by a Japanese national, who informed the temple. The bell was finally returned to Genkaku-ji in 1974, thirty-seven years after leaving. Next to the bell, the bodhisattva statue is a memorial to the dead of the South Pacific Islands (南洋群島物故者慰霊像) colonized by Japan. The shells scattered in front of the statue come from the waters around Saipan.

TOKYO WATERWORKS
HISTORICAL MUSEUM

Water from Edo

2-7-1 Hongo, Bunkyo-ku (東京都文京区本郷 2-7-1)
5-minute walk from Ochanomizu (御茶ノ水) or Shin-Ochanomizu
(新御茶ノ水) stations, JR Sobu or Chuo lines; Tokyo metro Marunouchi
or Chiyoda lines
Open 9.30am–5pm, closed fourth Monday of the month – if a public holiday
falls on a Monday the museum is open, but closed the following day; closed
28 December to 4 January
Admission free
English audio guide available; English-speaking guide for groups on reservation

Opened on this site in 1995 and renovated in 2009, this fascinating museum gives a comprehensiive history of the Tokyo water-supply system (東京都水道歴史館).

It covers one of the city's biggest challenges since the Edo era: the water supply of a megalopolis.

There are piles of antique wooden pipes, examples of the materials used for the modernization of the city in the Meiji period, and some impressive pipes from the current metropolis.

An actual water pumping station from the Edo period, excavated in 1982, is also on display. Outside is a reproduction of a section of the aqueduct that supplied Kanda.

Near the museum, a stone marks the site where the Kanda aqueduct crossed the Kandagawa over a bridge (掛樋 – *Kakehi*). It's also mentioned on another stele on Sotobori avenue, almost opposite the staff training centre for Tokyo Metropolis schools at 1-3 Hongo.

There are some remains of the Sekiguchi dam that regulated the flow near the Hotel Chinzanso in Edogawa Park (see p. 227).

Water for Edo

On his arrival in Edo in 1590, Ieyasu[1] launched the work to supply the town with drinking water, as the few wells near the bay couldn't meet the need, even if the water they drew wasn't too salty. After the first pipelines were laid (Koishikawa aqueduct), on which there remains little information, the shogunate built the Kanda aqueduct: 20 kilometres long and completed around 1629, it was designed to deliver spring water from Inokashira lake to Edo.

This aqueduct was used to supply Tokyo with drinking water until 1901, two years after the completion of the first modern distribution network.

The second major waterworks, Tamagawa aqueduct, dates from 1653. It brings water from the Tama to Yotsuya, 43 kilometres away, although the gradient is only around 100 metres. The upper part of this network is still in use.

After the Great Fire of Meireki in 1657, which destroyed two-thirds of the city (including the keep of Edo Castle, which was never re-built) and killed tens of thousands, the shogunate sought to bring more water into town and had another four aqueducts built, which in the end were only used for a few years.

---

[1] 徳川家康 *(Tokugawa Ieyasu), 1543–1616, 1ˢᵗ shogun of the Tokugawa dynasty.*

MON TILES OF THE AKAMON AT TODAI

Intruders at the gate

7-3-1 Hongo, Bunkyo-ku (東京都文京区本郷 7-3-1)
10 minutes from Todai-mae station (東大前), Tokyo metro Nanboku line;
or 10 minutes from Sanchome Hongo station (本郷三丁目), Tokyo metro
Marunouchi line; Toei subway Oedo line

The graceful Akamon (赤門 – Red Gate) of the University of Tokyo date from 1827, at the time when the Hongo campus was still the main residence of the Maeda clan of Kaga. It was built as a fitting welcome on the arrival of a new bride for the lord of the manor Maeda Nariyasu,[1] who took as his wife Yasuhime,[2] the 21th daughter of the 11th shogun, Tokugawa Ienari. The *mon* on the gate's tiles conceal an interesting curiosity.

You'll obviously find the emblems of the Tokugawa clan on the upper tiles and those of the Maeda clan below, but note the presence of intruders at the corner of the roof (level with the *onigawara* – 鬼瓦) and on the walls around the gate. On these few tiles, the "study" character was engraved with its old spelling (學 – *gaku*). If this character seems particularly well suited to the gates of a university, these tiles of course only date from the Edo era. The *onigawara* fell during the 1923 earthquake and was replaced in a style appropriate to the new functions of the site.

NEARBY
Phantom steps at Yayoi ⑫
Thirty-nine or forty steps?

In the 2-18 Yayoi neighbourhood just behind the Yayoi campus, a surprising flight of steps has been nicknamed the "ghost steps" (お化け階段). As you ascend, you count forty steps. On the way down – surprise! – you reach the ground after the thirty-ninth... The bottom step is particularly low, almost on the same level as the ground: going up, you're careful to set foot on this step and therefore count it. On the way down, it fools everyone.

University restaurants on the historic campus of Todai

The main campus of Todai, centre of excellence of Japanese universities, has three interconnected sections: the "historic" Hongo campus, the Yayoi campus occupied by the Faculty of Agriculture and the Earthquake Research Institute, and the smaller Asano campus behind Yayoi. The university canteens are open to the public and let you mix with the student population without denting your wallet. Each restaurant has its own reputation among students: some think that the catering at the Faculty of Agriculture at Yayoi is healthier; the impatient ones will mingle with the crowd in the huge Central Canteen (中央食堂) near the Yasuda auditorium; and purists will sample the *oyakodon* (chicken and egg rice), speciality of Icho Metro canteen (銀杏メトロ), former Canteen No. 1, in the basement of Building No. 2 of the Faculty of Law. Canteen No. 2 (第二食堂), which is rather quiet and well lit, also has its fans. Some large coffee chains have now opened on the campus. On the second floor of the Faculty House of Mukogaoka (向ヶ丘ファカルティハウス), opened in 2009 on the Yayoi campus, there's even a bar with an exclusive, subdued atmosphere comparable to some posh uptown establishments where the university staff or alumni come to cloud their minds.

Kototoi-dori avenue separates Yayoi campus from Asano and Hongo. Asano and Yayoi are a little newer than Hongo and rather less photogenic than their big brother. The stands of the baseball pitch north of Yayoi are nevertheless classed as an Important Cultural Property.

[1] 前田斉泰, *1811–1884, 12th and penultimate lord of the Maeda clan, one of the most powerful of the Edo period.*
[2] 溶姫, *1813–1868.*

Arakawa / Taito / Sumida

TRAMCARS ON THE ARAKAWA LINE

Rent-a-tram?

Waseda (早稲田) to Minowabashi (三ノ輪橋)
Car hire 10am–3.30pm
Reservations and enquiries: Metropolitan Government Bureau
of Transportation (東京都交通局)
Tel: 03-3893-7451 • www.kotsu.subway.tokyo.jp/toden/kanren/kashikiri.html

The Arakawa line offers an unfamiliar but enjoyable diversion – it's easy to book a tramcar for a day trip (with short stops at the stations), at a price that's very reasonable, even cheap, for a group. You can even choose the type of tramcar.

Arakawa, Tokyo's last surviving tramline

The Arakawa line (都電荒川線) is an often overlooked survivor of the extensive tram network operated by the local authorities that criss-crossed the city in the 1960s. Along with the Setagaya line, operated by Tokyu, this is the only line classified as a tramway still operating in Tokyo. Unlike the Setagaya, which runs on a dedicated track, the Arakawa line shares a small section of its route with road traffic – 500 metres between the Asukayama and Oji stops on Meiji-dori. So it could be said to be the only "real" city tram for barely half a kilometre.

The single tramcar threads its way into neighbourhoods of little houses in just over an hour between Minowa and Waseda, making it the ideal means of transport to serenely investigate 12 kilometres of deepest Tokyo north of Yamanote. This short ride, combined with a look around the trams at the depot, offers something of the atmosphere of post-war Tokyo, simple and no frills, away from the explosive neon experience of the city centre.

The depot covers an entire block at 8-33 Nishi-Ogu (nearest stop: Arakawa-Shako-Mae) in front of which a small square, *Toden Omoidehiroba* (都電おもいで広場 – Place of Remembrance), is free to the public. Two trams that were in use during the immediate post-war period are displayed together with a diorama of life in the 1950s.

ARAKAWA YUEN'S BRICK WALL ②

Remains of a former brickworks

6-34, 6-20, 6-21 Nishi-Ogu, Arakawa-ku (東京都荒川区西尾久 6-34, 6-21, 6-20)
5 minutes from Arakawa-yuenchimae station (荒川遊園地 前), Toei Arakawa streetcar

Not far from Arakawa Yuen Park, some old red-brick walls blend into the background on the site of a former brickworks dating from the early 20th century.

The north of Arakawa along the Sumida River used to be an industrial zone, where the first suburbs grew up together with the first factory chimneys of the Meiji era. A few workshops scattered here and there among the narrow streets are a reminder that the area has not become exclusively residential.

From the early Meiji years, four brickworks stood along the riverbank, benefiting from easy access to the city.

This curious wall over 200 metres long is a relic of one of the brickworks, Hirooka, which opened in 1895 and burned down in 1921.

A good part of the site was, however, given another lease of life: in 1922 it was rehabilitated as a private leisure park (for want of a better word), Arakawa Yuen (あらかわ遊園), with a cinema, restaurants and tearoom.

There are several amusement parks within the city, the well-known Hanayashiki top of the list. Arakawa Yuen on the banks of the Sumida, now the only public park directly managed by the district, is much less well known but will delight the under-10s. In almost a century of history, the park has changed a great deal, going from private to public, and it now includes several smaller attractions, simple, resourceful, unpretentious.

NEARBY
Oku station toilets ③

The name of JR East railway station, opened in 1929 to serve what used to be the village of Ogu (尾久村), reads "Oku" rather than Ogu. The main curiosity of this station, one of the least used of the JR East Tokyo network, is the appearance of the public toilets in the parking space in front of the station, at 1-2-17 Showamachi.

In a rather striking design for a station of this type, a little building forms the letters O K U. The women's facilities are in the O, men's in the U, and disabled in the K. The building stands just behind the *koban* and a *convenience store*, but once near the gates it's hard to miss, on the east side of the car park.

Ogu village was a rustic suburban outpost of the early 20th century, mixing *ryotei, ryokan* and even some *onsens*, a retreat eventually absorbed into the metropolis. The heart of it lay around Odai, Miyanomae and Kumanomae tram stations.

A hot spring was discovered and exploited from 1914. Geisha roamed the neighbourhood until the 1960s, although the post-war industrial boom and the gradual drying-up of the springs harmed Ogu, the final blow being when the economic bubble burst.

There are a few restaurants and *ryotei* but no traditional *ryokan*, and nothing or little of the glorious buzz of yesteryear. Ogu has been eaten up and digested by the rest of the city and now exudes tranquillity.

GRAVES OF DISSECTED BODIES AT YANAKA

Thousands of bodies left to science

7-16 Yanaka, Taito-ku (東京都台東区谷中 7-16)
5-minute walk from Nippori station (日暮里), JR Yamanote, Keihin-Tohoku,
Joban, Keisei Honsen lines; Toei subway; Nippori-Toneri Liner • Open 24/7

In the tombs section of Tenno-ji (地蔵尊前横断), on the north side of Yanaka cemetery, about 50 metres to the right as you enter the rows of tombs via the path starting opposite the Jizo in front of the temple, you'll see three tombs bearing the engraving *Senninzuka* (千人塚 – Stele of a Thousand Persons). Erected in 1881, 1892 and 1913 respectively, each grave marker is dedicated to 1,000 people who were dissected for scientific research at the University of Tokyo's Faculty of Medicine.

Note the peculiar spelling of the character used for the word "stele" (*zuka*, normally 塚 but here 冢), which does not hold the key to the earth (土). The omission is deliberate, signifying that the bodies were not returned to the earth, but have been used for science. On the sides of the tombstones, time-worn inscriptions recall the origin of these graves.

A little west of the three stelae, an elegant little pagoda stands over an ossuary for the remains of dissections from the Faculty of Medicine until 1875. The beginnings of the study of anatomy at the University of Tokyo were down to Taguchi Kazuyoshi,[1] one of the country's first medical doctors and author of the first original Japanese treatises on anatomy. Taguchi, absorbed in his dissections, was reputed to be very detached from the outside world: for example, it's said that he wasn't even aware of the first Sino-Japanese War (1894–1895) until the signing of the Treaty of Shimonoseki on 17 April 1895.

"Hill to Mount Fuji"

Farther north of Yanaka cemetery, the shopping street of Yanaka Ginza with its traditional shops leads to Nippori station. The street is broken up by a flight of steps (夕やけだんだん – Yuyake Dandan), renowned for its view of the setting sun as much as for the many feral cats lying around. Yanaka Ginza, despite its somewhat antiquated look, was only properly developed after the war. Near the steps, the temple enclosure of Hoko-ji is known as the Hill to Mount Fuji (富士見坂). This is one of the few places in Yamanote where Mount Fuji could be seen from Tokyo, except from a skyscraper. But by mid-2013 the residential expansion to the west had unfortunately blocked much of the view.

[1] 田口和義, *1839-1904.*

BINBO GA SARU STATUE ⑤

A temple statue inspired by a video game

1-5-34 Yanaka, Taito-ku (東京都台東区谷中 1-5-34)
10-minute walk from Nezu station (根津), Tokyo metro Chiyoda line
Cemetery open 9am–5pm daily

I n the heart of the traditional streets of Yanaka and among its many temples, worshippers and visitors to Myosen-ji are greeted by an extremely unusual statue entitled *Binbo ga saru zo* (貧乏が去る像 – Statue of Departing Poverty).

The statue represents a Binbogami (貧乏神), spirit of poverty, with a monkey (猿 – *saru*) on top. The name of this statue is a pun, as *saru* also means "leave".

To chase away the Binbogami that lurks in everyone, you must first caress the statue of Binbogami and then the monkey.

The design of the statue, erected in 2003, reprises the Binbogami series of video games, *Momotaro Dentetsu*. It was even used to promote the twelfth instalment of the series.

The temple was opened in the 17th century, but this statue is proof that Buddhism can adapt to current trends when necessary. Piggy banks in the same style are on sale.

Momotaro Dentetsu

Virtually unknown outside Japan, this franchise based on a video game released in 1988 for Famicom (NES in Europe) has released over twenty episodes in the domestic market, and has been adapted to many consoles, not to mention mobile phones.

The game, with its comic graphics, is similar to a board game where each player must get rich by travelling on Japanese public transport.

ABANDONED STATION OF KEISEI HAKUBUTSUKAN-DOBUTSUEN

A station with accumulated problems

13-23 Ueno-koen, Taito-ku (東京都台東区上野公園 13-23)
10 minutes from Ueno (上野) and Keisei Ueno (京成上野) stations, JR
Yamanote, Keihin-Tohoku or Joban Utsunomiya lines; Tokyo metro Ginza,
Hibiya, Shinkansen or Keisei Honsen lines
Accessible 24/7

The small building with the pyramidal roof next to the Tokyo National Museum in Ueno leads to the underground station of Keisei Hakubutsukan-Dobutsuen (京成博物館動物園 – Museum and Zoo), opened in 1933.

Despite a location that seems attractive on paper, attendance has been falling over the years. Too close to the massive Ueno, poorly served by local trains, too short to accommodate the long carriages of modern trains, the station had accumulated problems.

It no longer received trains from 1997, before being finally abandoned in 2004. The bronze lamp seen on the beautiful façade of the building was restored in 2010.

Underground, this section of the line is dimly lit with neon lights. The platforms, with their walls partially painted yellow, are still clearly visible to the left from the trains. You can also easily spot the entrances and some signs for passengers. The station building is closed and the platforms are not normally accessible.

KOREAN BUSINESSES IN MIKAWASHIMA ⑦

An authentic touch of Korea in Tokyo

*3 Higashi-Nippori, Arakawa-ku (東京都荒川区東日暮里 3) and around
Mikawashima station (三河島), JR Joban line
Accessible 24/7*

Several Korean restaurants and shops selling goods from the Land of the Morning Calm can be found south of Mikawashima station, especially in the shopping streets of Shinkokubo (親交睦商店街). In those few institutions with their *Hangul* signs,[1] grilled meat and *kimchi* (traditional fermented vegetables), is no gimmick but a taste of the authentic memory of the country.

North of the station, towards 1-4-22 Nishi-Nippori, a speciality shop sells kimchi, meat and other condiments in an atmosphere reminiscent of the markets of old Seoul.

KAN'EIJI-SAKA ⑧

Another abandoned station on the Keisei line

Just 500 metres after Keisei Hakubutsukan-Dobutsuen, at 2-4-6 Ueno-Sakuragi, an old warehouse is actually the Kan'eiji-saka station building (寛永寺坂), which served Kan'eiji, one of the two *bodaiji* (Buddhist "bodhi temple") of Tokugawa. Like Hakubutsukan-Dobutsuen, the station was opened in 1933 but abandoned in 1953 (trains had no longer stopped there since 1947). Nowadays the station square is parking space. Underground, the platforms have gone, the train passes fairly quickly and the lighting is low, but a keen eye on the Keisei line train between Keisei Ueno and Nippori may notice changes in the patterns of the walls with their wood-panelled base. From Nippori towards Ueno on the Keisei line, the station appears a few seconds after the train enters the tunnel.

There are other stations and abandoned platforms in Tokyo, notably at Omotesando (see p. 46) and Manseibashi (p. 19).

---

[1] *Korean alphabet.*

FACE OF THE GREAT BUDDHA OF UENO

A Buddha to help you pass your exams

4-8 Ueno-koen, Taito-ku (東京都台東区上野公園 4-8)
5-minute walk from Ueno (上野) and Keisei Ueno (京成上野) stations; JR Yamanote, Keihin-Tohoku, Joban or Utsunomiya lines; Tokyo metro Ginza, Hibiya, Shinkansen or Keisei Honsen lines
Accessible 9am–3pm

oncealed among the trees of Ueno Park, near the bell (*Toki no Kane* – 時の鐘, see also p. 21), behind the Gojoten shrine, is a vast carving of the face of Buddha.

This plump and compassionate figure is all that remains of the Great Buddha of Ueno (上野大仏), which dominated the area from its 6-metre height until 1923.

An earlier plaster statue almost 3 metres high had been installed in 1631 by Hori Naoyori,[1] lord of the lands around Niigata, to appease the war dead. It was destroyed in the 1647 earthquake.

A new and larger bronze statue was erected in the late 17th century. In 1841, a fire destroyed the building that sheltered the statue and it was damaged. Despite speedy restoration work, next time it was the head that fell off in an 1855 earthquake before being restored once again. The building that protected the statue was dismantled in 1873 when Ueno Park was opened to the public. The head of the statue fell one last time in the Great Kanto Earthquake of 1923, and the body and support were melted down for the war effort. The Buddha's face was finally installed on its current base in 1972. Below the face you'll find two photographs of the statue in the days when it was still intact.

Touching this statue apparently brings good luck – surviving the test of time four times (admittedly with limited success) has earned the statue the nickname, "Great Buddha of Success" (合格大仏), hence the occasional visits of students preparing for their exams.

---

[1] 堀直寄, *1577–1639.*

CENOTAPH FOR THE ANIMALS OF UENO ZOO

Animals, rest in peace

9-83 Ueno-koen, Taito-ku (東京都台東区上野公園 9-83), Ueno Zoo
10 minutes from Ueno (上野) and Keisei Ueno (京成上野) stations, JR Yamanote, Keihin-Tohoku, Joban or Utsunomiya lines; Tokyo metro Ginza, Hibiya, Shinkansen or Keisei Honsen lines
Open 9.30am–5pm daily, closed 29 December to 1 January, closed on Mondays (with exceptions) – if a public holiday falls on a Monday the zoo is open, but closed the following day

Next to the elephant enclosure of Japan's oldest zoo, the memorial to its dead animals (動物慰霊碑) replaces the first memorial erected in 1931 next to the gibbons' cage.

Today's version, with its ribbon and its owl, dates from 1975, the year the zoo was renovated. The ribbon symbolizes affection for animals, while the owl protects the spirits of the dead beasts. Under the monument is engraved the inscription, *Dobutsuyo, yasurakani* (動物よ安らかに – Animals, rest in peace).

The board in front of the memorial is often elaborately decorated, as schoolchildren sometimes leave origami or colourful messages.

Poisoned, starved or strangled ...

The first memorial commemorated the animals killed during the war, among others.

In August 1943, because of the danger of animals escaping from their cages after the bombing, the Metropolitan Government ordered the zoo to put down its residents. Twenty-seven animals of various species (python, bear, lion, etc.) that were considered dangerous were then poisoned, starved or strangled, allegedly to avoid shooting them, which could have scared civilians. A short ceremony was held in September 1943.

The tragic fate of the three mascot elephants John, Wanly and Tonky, which were starved to death, was even the subject of a children's book after the war. Other animals, including hippos, also starved to death after the 1945 bombing. Ueno Zoo took years to recover.

NEARBY
The police station and mailbox at Ueno Zoo ⑪

The Ueno *Zoo koban*, built in 1990 by architect Kurokawa Tetsuro,[1] a few metres from the entrance and ticket offices, is a rather surprising geometric construction. Standing in the middle of the park – with its many unmissable national museums and other historic attractions – this highly original *koban*, inspired by the forest and wood (杜 – *mori*), goes almost unnoticed.

The same goes for the black and white mailbox in the shape of a panda installed at the entrance to the zoo in 2011. It's extremely lifelike: the back of the box even has a little tail.

[1] 黒川哲郎, *1943–2013.*

MUMMIFIED *KAPPA* ARM AT SOGEN-JI

Kappa *everywhere*

In the Kappa-do of the temple
3-7-2 Matsugaya, Taito-ku (東京都台東区松が 谷 3-7-2)
10 minutes from Asakusa station (浅草), Tokyo metro Ginza line, Toei subway Asakusa line; Isezaki (Tobu Skytree Line)
Open 9am–5pm
To see the Kappa-do where the mummy is stored, ask at the temple at least the day before
Tel: 03-3841-2035

Almost halfway through the chequerboard of alleys and streets between Ueno and Asakusa, near Kappabashi avenue and its kitchen utensils, Sogen-ji keeps a so-called "mummified *kappa* arm" (see box).

The mummified limb of the legendary creature, discovered by chance in the early 20th century in a warehouse, was bequeathed to the temple. The cover of the protective box says this is the arm of a *suiko* (水虎),

generally regarded as a particular kind of *kappa*. You can clearly see the crooked fingers and nails on the little white hand.

The arm is displayed in the Kappa-do, a small annex to the temple, where you'll also find all manner of goodies and drawings relating to the *kappa*, including some authentic drawings by manga masters, beginning with Tezuka Osamu.[1] The *kappa*'s hand is visible from the outside, but you should ask at the temple (at least the day before your visit) to go inside the Kappa-do and see drawings on the ceiling. Visits are accompanied.

The *kappa*, as everyone knows, is a big fan of cucumbers. The offerings box in front of the Kappa-do is sometimes covered with the vegetables...

Inside the temple are other *kappa* statues, including (next to the entrance) a fairly artistic slender statue entitled *Kappa no Gichan* (かっぱのぎーちゃん – Gichan the kappa). Its long stone face is clearly on the border between cucumber and kappa.

Sogen-ji was founded in the late 16th century and moved to its present site in the mid-17th century. The temple's association with the legendary creature dates from the early 19th century, when the tomb of a wealthy local merchant called Kihachi Kappaya[2] was installed there. Using his own funds, Kihachi had launched excavations for the Shinhorikawa canal to help protect the low-lying area from recurrent flooding, to the delight of local residents. According to legend, Kihachi had saved a *kappa* from the Sumida River and the *kappas* had then helped him to complete the difficult construction work. Kihachi's tomb is at the very foot of the Kappa-do steps. Inside, next to the mummified arm, is an illustration of the legend of the *kappas* helping Kihachi and an old photograph of the neighbourhood when the canal was under construction. You'll also find a golden statue commemorating the legend at 2-25-9 Matsugaya.

The kappa (河童)

Mythical river creature, often depicted in a humanoid or ape-like form, often a mischievous prankster, sometimes evil and dangerous, the *kappa* is one of the most representative figures of Japanese folklore. Numerous *kappa* mummies date back to the Edo period and actually use the remains of otters or combinations of various animals.

---

[1] 手塚治虫, *1928–1989, one of the most influential manga artists in Japan, author among others of* Astroboy, Kimba the White Lion *and* Black Jack.
[2] 合羽屋喜八, ?–1814.

BURNED TREES AT SENSO-JI

Survivors of the 1945 bombing

2-3-1 Asakusa, Taito-ku (東京都台東区浅草 2-3-1)
5-minute walk from Asakusa station (浅草), Tokyo metro Ginza line, Toei
subway Asakusa line; Isezaki (Tobu Skytree Line)
Temple precinct accessible 24/7

Inside the walls of the famous Senso-ji at Asakusa, over a dozen trees survived the bombardment of March 1945 although this temple, the city's oldest, was almost razed to the ground.

The scars on these few forgotten survivors are testimony to the violence of the event.

The most obvious is a large ginkgo tree standing a few metres southwest of the *hondo* rebuilt in 1958, just in front of the police box next to the Nitenmon door.

The tree seems very healthy, but if you look carefully at the trunk you'll see blackened traces of the burns inflicted in 1945.

Other trees have suffered the same fate in the temple, for example those in front of the five-storey pagoda or just behind the *hondo*. You'll notice striking contrasts in the state of some of their trunks: on the burned part of the tree the trunk is raw and smooth, while the part that grew after the war is generally covered with rough bark.

The trees most likely to have survived are certainly old enough to have lived through the war. So look for the broadest trunks to find the bruised trees and escape from the crowds for a few moments.

YOKOAMICHO PARK

One of the city's most poignant commemorative sites

2-3-25 Yokoami Sumida, Tokyo (東京都墨田区横網 2-3-25)
5-minute walk from Ryogoku station (両国), JR Sobu or Chuo line,
Toei subway Oedo line
Park accessible 24/7
Museum open 9am–5pm every day except Monday – if a public holiday
falls on a Monday the museum is open, but closed the following day; closed
29 December to 3 January

Yokoamicho-koen (横網町公園), not far from the National Sumo Stadium, doesn't look anything special yet it's one of the city's most significant and deeply moving parks. A walk through it, along a rarely visited route except for the remembrance ceremonies (10 March for the victims of the bombing, 1 September for the earthquake), won't leave you indifferent.

The "spiritual memorial" of Tokyo Metropolis is an elegant 1930s building surmounted by a pagoda.

The park is the site of a massacre: on 1 September 1923, tens of thousands of Tokyoites found refuge there after the Great Kanto Earthquake, when the park was still under construction. Surrounded by flames triggered by the earthquake, it was swiftly engulfed in a firestorm. Some 38,000 people perished in the park alone, almost half of the Tokyo victims of the earthquake.

The memorial erected in 1930 was designed by Ito Chuta,[1] architect of Hongan-ji at Tsukiji. The ashes of 58,000 earthquake victims were placed in the temple pagoda, which served as an ossuary.

Fifteen years later, on the night of 9–10 March 1945, Operation Meetinghouse was responsible for another 100,000 victims in the deadliest air raid of World War II, and the history of the world, before Hiroshima, Nagasaki and Dresden (see p. 253).

The bodies hastily buried in the city parks were eventually disinterred and cremated in 1948. Their ashes were placed at the memorial, which is now the final resting place for over 160,000 victims of the city's great disasters.

Just in front of the memorial, a monument dedicated to victims of the bombing preserves the names of the dead.

The park also has a stone commemorating the Koreans who were massacred by mobs and militias after the 1923 earthquake, when they were seen as the root of all evil.

On the outskirts of the park, the Kanto Earthquake Memorial Museum (東京都復興記念館) deals primarily with the effects of the earthquake, but also has some exhibits on the great bombardment. It's free, poignant and raw.

---

[1] 伊東忠太, *1867-1954. Historian and architect, also responsible for the Heian Jingu shrine at Kyoto and the reconstruction of Yushima Seido (Yushima sacred hall, a Confucian temple from the Edo period) in Tokyo's Bunkyo ward.*

LAKE OF THE FORMER YASUDA GARDENS

Pump that mimics the movement of the tides

1-12-1 Yokoami, Sumida-ku (東京都墨田区横網 1-12-1)
5 minutes from Ryogoku station (両国), JR Sobu line; Toei subway Oedo or Chuo lines
Open 9am–4.30pm daily, except 29 December to 1 January; open until 6pm in June, July and August (except Sumida fireworks day)
Admission free

The former Yasuda gardens (旧安田庭園), on the site of a stately home acquired by the Meiji contractor Yasuda Zenjiro,[1] are neither extensive nor sublime, but refined enough to merit a detour – after attending a sumo match, for example.

The lake was linked to the Sumida River in the Edo period and a pump installed to reproduce tidal movements, subtly changing the appearance of the waters in the heart of the gardens according to the time of day.

In one corner, the elegant, circular Ryogokukoukaido building (両国公会堂) used to be reflected in the lake.

Dating from the Taisho era and used as an entertainment venue during the Allied Occupation, its questionable resistance to earthquakes led to its demolition in 2015.

Honjo, a twice-battered district

Sumida ward resulted from the 1947 merger between the districts of Honjo and Mukojima. Honjo, to the south, was the easternmost district of Tokyo during the Meiji period, and was almost annihilated on two occasions: in 1923 during the Great Kanto Earthquake, and in 1945 when incendiary bombs rained down on the city. The Dai-ichi Hotel Ryogoku stands on the site of the former town hall.

---

[1] 安田善次郎, *1838-1921. Founder of the 19ᵗʰ century Yasuda zaibatsu, one of the most powerful in the country until it was disbanded after the war. Mizuho Bank is an offshoot.*

SUMIDA HERITAGE MUSEUM

Rediscover the importance of the river

2-3-5 Mukojima, Sumida-ku (東京都墨田区向島 2-3-5)
*10-minute walk from Tokyo Skytree / Oshiage station (とうきょうスカイツ
リー/押上), Isezaki (Tobu Skytree Line); Tokyo metro Hanzomon line; Toei
subway Asakusa, Keisei Oshiage or Keisei Honsen lines*
*Open 9am–5pm every day except Monday – if a public holiday falls on a
Monday the museum is open, but closed the following day; closed fourth
Wednesday of the month – if a public holiday falls on a Wednesday the
museum is open, but closed the following day; closed 29 December to 2 January*

At the entrance to Kenban-dori, Sumida Heritage Museum (すみだ郷土文化資料館), at 2-3-5 Mukojima, is run by the local authority. Sumida is perhaps not Tokyo's most historically significant ward, but the Sumida River holds a key place in the city, hence the interest of this small museum.

The river has been twinned since October 1989 with the Seine, which speaks volumes about its closeness to the hearts of Tokyoites. The river, which served as the border between Musashi and Shimousa provinces until the 17th century, is rich in anecdotes and symbols.

The museum provides fascinating details about life by the river, and

the historic role of the Azuma Bridge opposite Asakusa, and summarizes the damage caused by the incendiary bombing of 1945. The main exhibitions can be covered in half an hour or so, but with the small admission fee you won't regret a visit.

Discreet *kagai* of *Mukojima*

Kyoto is better known abroad for the traditional female entertainers known as geisha (literally "art person"), but Tokyo has its own, more discreet, version. The Mukojima *kagai* ("flower towns") are home to a dozen *ryotei* (upmarket restaurants) concentrated in the streets around Kenban-dori, which employ a hundred or so geisha. Mukojima is in fact the liveliest of the city's "flower and willow worlds". The various establishments are fairly easy to spot: more or less traditional buildings with a friendly, comfortable look amid rather ageing 1990s buildings, from Futaba (ふ多葉) in the north, to Kiyoshi (きよし), Irifune (入舟), Sakurachaya (櫻茶ヤ), Namimura (波むら) and Sumida (すみ多) in the south.

List of ryoteis

Name	Location (Mukojima Sumida-ku) 東京都墨田区向島
Chiyoda (千代田)	5-20-13
Futaba (ふ多葉)	5-24-13
Hananosato (花の里)	5-13-18
Ichimatsu (壱松)	2-8-13
Ichiyama (市山)	5-28-4
Irifune (入舟)	5-28-5
Kiyoshi (きよし)	5-35-3
Miyako (美家古)	5-3-5
Namimura (波むら)	2-15-8
Sakurachaya (櫻茶ヤ)	5-24-10
Sensui (千穂)	2-9-3
Sumida (すみ多)	2-15-13
Tsukibue (月笛)	5-29-9

SHIRAHIGE-HIGASHI *DANCHI*

The giant Sumida firewall

Tsutsumi-dori, Sumida-ku (東京墨田区堤通)
10-minute walk from Higashi-Mukojima (東向島) or Kanegafuchi (鐘ヶ淵)
stations, Isezaki (Tobu Skytree Line)
Accessible 24/7

Shirahige-Higashi *danchi* (白鬚東アパート), towards the north of the ward, is known as the "Great Wall of Sumida". It consists of a row over 1½ kilometres long of eighteen gigantic and gloomy thirteen-storey residential blocks, built in the 1970s. The semi-detached buildings form a solid wall opposite the Sumida River, on the other side of Higashi-Shirahige Park.

The blocks were in fact built as a vast firewall between the downtown

neighbourhood of Mukojima and the park. North Sumida, packed with older wooden buildings, is considered a disaster risk area and the park is designated as the evacuation zone for 80,000 residents who would be vulnerable to any catastrophic fire. There's no question of north Sumida turning into an inferno from which nobody could escape, as Tokyo has experienced enough of that kind of destruction in its history.

The Great Wall is all the more impressive when you notice the little details that make up the firewall. The few ground-floor corridors between the various buildings are protected by thick fire doors, while the entrances and windows are fitted with rolling steel shutters. Hoses and red fire cannons can be seen around the walls and on the balconies.

The *danchi*, a monument to disaster prevention, is beginning to show its age. As Shirahige-Higashi has never been used as a firewall, its effectiveness remains to be seen, but it's unique in Tokyo.

THE SEIKO MUSEUM

Story time

3-9-7 Higashi Mukojima, Sumida-ku (東京都墨田区東向島 3-9-7)
10 minutes from Higashi-Mukojima (東向島) or Kanegafuchi (鐘ヶ淵)
stations; Isezaki (Tobu Skytree Line)
Open 10am–4pm, closed Mondays and public holidays (open 3, 4 and 5 May)
and for year-end holidays – if a public holiday falls on a Monday, the museum
is closed the following day too
Free guided tours

Until 1999, The Seiko Museum (セイコーミュージアム) was located on its original production site at Kinsicho (the quasi-mythical Seikosha watch factory that shaped life to the north of the station). Following the closure of the factory, it moved into a former warehouse, away from the centre.

The museum (founded in 1881) covers the measurement of time and the history of the company. Displayed over two floors are hundreds of clocks and watches of all kinds.

The tour begins on the first floor with some historical artefacts, from sundials to ingenious analogue devices that, for example, measure the passage of time with running water. Several antique mechanical clocks are on display. The information boards (mainly in Japanese) give a layman's view of the physical phenomena behind quartz pulsations. The second floor gives a detailed review of 20th century history as seen through the prism of Seiko and its watches. From the first mechanical watches of the early 20th century, watches melted in the fire following the 1923 earthquake, watches in war, the first quartz watches, GPS watches and watches of the future, the museum travels through time and its measurement.

At the end of the tour, just before the exit, you'll see some examples of stopwatches from the world of sport.

Although in theory visits are only on reservation, the museum welcomes the occasional visitor without too many problems, as the site is far from being overwhelmed by crowds. Although the minor promotional aspect is sometimes annoying, the museum is sufficiently inventive to satisfy the curious, with stimulating explanations from the tour guides.

IMADO SHRINE

Maybe the source of maneki-neko?

1-5-22 Imado, Taito-ku (東京台東区今戸 1-5-22)
10-minute walk from Asakusa station (浅草), Tokyo metro Ginza line, Toei
subway Asakusa line
Open 9am–5pm

A few minutes' walk north, away from Asakusa's crowds of tourists, the precincts of the Imado shrine (今戸神社) offer a unique haven of tranquillity near the banks of the Sumida.

The shrine was founded in the 11th century, although the current building dates from the 1970s. It claims to be the source of the ceramic figurines called *maneki-neko* (literally "beckoning cat", a common good-luck charm), a status disputed with Gotoku-ji, a temple in Setagaya (see p. 99).

Legend has it that in the 16th century a cat appeared at this spot in the dreams of a poor woman, inviting her to make (and sell) ceramic cats. Unsurprisingly, the invitation bore fruit even if it took until 2007 for the shrine to erect a commemorative stone topped by two cats that visitors can (or must) stroke. Another stele celebrates the beginnings of Imado ceramics.

At the same time, the Imado shrine is dedicated to the divine couple Izanagi and his sister/wife Izanami, the first married couple in the Shinto pantheon. Riding on this wave, the shrine is well positioned in the niche market where the search for love is paramount: young women (and men) often go there to pray for a partner. The shrine even organizes "meet your soulmate" events.

Combining the two traditions, the shrine is now dominated by the symbolism of the feline couple.

Imado, Danzaemon and the lowly castes

Some outcast communities gathered north of Asakusa on the outskirts of Edo, almost to the waters of today's Sumida River, at the time of the shoguns. They included the Eta (穢多), who carried out the most impure tasks, such as dealing with dead animals, and the *hinin* (非人 – "non-humans"), on the lowest rungs of the social ladder. On the site of Asakusa's Metropolitan High School, beside the Imado shrine, was the residence of the Danzaemon (弾左衛門), a hereditary position to keep an eye on these "sub-humans" on behalf of the shogunate in the Tokyo region. Castes were abolished in the Meiji period, and the 1923 earthquake and World War II largely ended that state of affairs.

MEMORIAL TO YOSHIWARA PROSTITUTES AT JOKAN-JI

20

Bodies of prostitutes wrapped in straw ...

2-1-12 Minamisenju, Arakawa-ku (東京都荒川区南千住 2-1-12)
5-minute walk from Minowa station (三ノ輪), Tokyo metro Hibiya line
Open 8am–5pm

Jokan-ji (浄閑寺), a temple dating from 1655 near Minowa subway station, just west of Minami-Senju on the Joban railway line, is the

final resting place of some 20,000 prostitutes from Yoshiwara district (see below). Behind the temple, a stele below a simple memorial commemorates the plight of these women with a poem: *Umarete ha kukai, shishite ha Jokanji* (生まれては苦界、死しては浄閑寺 – Born in suffering, in death at Jokan-ji).

The temple was a *Nage-komi dera* (投げ込寺 – Dumping Temple), where it was acceptable to dispose of the dead bodies of Yoshiwara prostitutes by laying them at the door of the temple, sometimes wrapped in rice straw.

Otherwise they would become *Muen-botoke* (無縁仏 – Buddha without Connections): the dead with no family or friends to perform the usual burial rites or to visit and maintain the graves and make their offerings.

The memorial dates from 1930, the successor to a votive stele of 1855 commemorating the death of about 500 prostitutes in an earthquake. The number of offerings at the memorial shows that the thousands of Yoshiwara prostitutes aren't completely forgotten by modern Tokyo.

San'ya Bori and Yoshiwara

Yoshiwara, the home of prostitution institutionalized by the shogunate in the 17th century and governed by a set of very strict rules, was one of the main red-light districts of the Edo period, especially as neighbourhood "rivals" were banned over the years. Hundreds of prostitutes and courtesans classified by their "quality" were made available to clients in nearly 150 establishments (遊女屋 – *yujoya*), concentrated in a few blocks from where they weren't allowed to stray. There was private access by boat via the San'ya Bori canal, which flowed between the Minowa and Sumida rivers but gradually silted up in the 20th century.

The avenue of Dote-dori was covered over with a dyke[1] that ran alongside the canal to protect the city from flooding if the Sumida burst its banks. To the south, both banks of the canal were built up. The little San'ya Bori Park alongside the Sumida marks the beginning of the canal. Dote-dori goes as far as 4-Senzoku, which along with 3-Senzoku is Yoshiwara's address today, through the district's historic gate of Yoshiwara-Daimon.

---

[1] *In Japanese,* tsutsumi *(堤), hence the name of the district,* Nihon-Zutsumi *(日本堤).*

21

JOE'S STATUE AT SAN'YA

Reinvigorating the Tokyo doya-gai

1-32 Nihon-Zutsumi, Taito-ku (東京都台東区日本堤 1-32)
10-minute walk from Minami-Senju station (南千住), Tokyo metro Hibiya
line, JR Joban line, MIR Tsukuba express
Accessible 24/7

At the entrance to Iroha shopping precinct on the Yoshiwara side, near 1-32 Nihon-Zutsumi, a statue of Yabuki Joe almost 2 metres tall makes you think that the hero of the legendary boxing manga *Ashita no Joe* (Tomorrow's Joe) is wandering nonchalantly along Date-dori, hands in pockets, plaster on cheek and jacket slung over shoulder. The facial features and hairstyle stick close to the manga, but the statue's proportions and realistic look can be deceptive from a distance.

With its punning name (立つんだ像, *Tatsunda-zo* – "standing statue", which sounds like *tatsunda, Joe* – "get up, Joe"), the reinforced plastic statue unveiled in late 2012 is the result of the precinct's efforts to try and (re)invigorate the neighbourhood, which served as backdrop to the manga in the 1960s and 70s.

San'ya: the nearest thing to a ghetto of human misery

San'ya (山谷), the neighbourhood where Joe wanders around, no longer features in the district names on city maps. Asakusa-San'ya existed until 1966 but has been divided up, renamed and absorbed by the three neighbouring districts of Kiyokawa, Nihon-Zutsumi and Higashi-Asakusa. San'ya is historically the Tokyo *doya-gai*: the last-resort refuge for vagrants, the homeless and casual labourers, packed with small establishments offering unserviced rooms for the night, *kan-i-shukusho* (簡易宿所 – literally "basic accommodation"). You don't live in San'ya, you just exist. In the 1960s there were over 15,000 workers living from hand to mouth, doing the most menial tasks to support the country's explosive development. The government's family housing projects implemented throughout the 1960s and 70s moved the women and children away and gradually transformed San'ya into a zone of single and impoverished men. Although the number of day labourers is now significantly less, San'ya has kept its poor reputation and rather run-down appearance – the nearest thing to a ghetto of human misery in the city. The neighbourhood has greatly aged by now and the number of solitary elderly men, too old to work, has markedly increased. The best they can hope for is to die peacefully on a tatami mat in one of the tiny rented rooms.

CONVERTED TAMANOI CAFÉS ㉒

In the alleys of 3 Sumida, Sumida-ku (東京都墨田区墨田 3)
10 minutes from Higashi-Mukojima station (東向島),
Isezaki (Tobu Skytree Line)
Accessible 24/7

In the middle of blocks of houses at 3 Sumida, you can still see some unusual, rather curvaceous buildings. These old "cafés" are actually brothels that reopened after the war, and have since been converted into individual homes. The unusual architecture was designed to draw attention to the houses in order to attract passing trade.

Good examples are the house with walls rounded at the corners towards 3-2-15 Sumida, a few houses around 3-14-7 and others at 3-12. Mosaic tiles are still visible on some walls, remains of their typically whimsical decoration.

REMAINS OF KOZUKAPPARA EXECUTION SITE

Torture at Edo's northern gates

2-34-5 Minami-Senju, Arakawa-ku (東京都荒川区南千住区 2-34-5)
Minami-Senju station (南千住), Tokyo metro Hibiya line, JR Joban line, MIR
Tsukuba express

Kozukappara (小塚原刑場) in Minami-Senju district, on the fringes of the city during the Edo period, was one of two main execution sites, the other being Suzugamori (see p. 66). Until it was shut down by the Meiji, 200,000 people lost their lives in various often public executions (burning at the stake, beheading, crucifixion, impalement... depending on the gravity of their crime).

Despite these vast numbers of executions, the field has few traces. Today, a 4-metre statue of Jizo in Enmei-ji, the temple at the west exit of Minami-Senju station, commemorates the site. This Jizo, who managed to keep his head, ended up as the "Jizo of decapitation".

Ironically, the Joban railway line cut through what was the execution field in the late 19th century. The Jizo statue and the cemetery, which had suffered significant damage during the 2011 earthquake, were restored in 2012.

Enmei-ji is now stuck between two tracks. North of the line is the cemetery of Minamisenju-Ekoin temple, which takes up the other half of the field. This temple was built in 1667 to appease the spirits of execution victims. Some of the victims of the Great Purge of Ansei at the end of the shogunate (1854–1860) are also buried in the cemetery. A decorative stele on one of the temple walls commemorates the visit in 1771 of three *rangakushas* (Japanese intellectuals who studied foreign science), Sugita Genpaku,[1] Nagakawa Jun'an[2] and Maeno Ryotaku.[3] Having observed the dissection of the executed victims, the three scientists translated *Ontleedkundige Tafelen*, the Dutch version of a German medical treatise, the first textbook to be fully translated from a Western language into Japanese. Their work led to the publication of *Kaitai Shinsho* (解体新書 – New Anatomy Treatise).

In the cemetery itself, note the original tomb of Ude no Kisaburo[4] in the shape of an arm. Kisaburo was an Edo warrior who, when he was wounded in one arm in a battle, hacked off the rest of the limb himself. The neighbouring grave is that of Takahashi Oden,[5] the last woman to be beheaded in Japan, in 1879.

Farther south, prisoners crossed to Kozukappara via the appropriately named Namidabashi (泪橋 – literally "Bridge of Tears").

[1] 杉田玄白, *1733-1817.*
[2] 中川 淳庵, *1739-1786.*
[3] 前野良沢, *1723-1803.*
[4] 腕の喜三郎, *1642-1715.*
[5] 高橋お伝, *1850–1879, executed for cutting the throat of a man who refused to lend her money.*

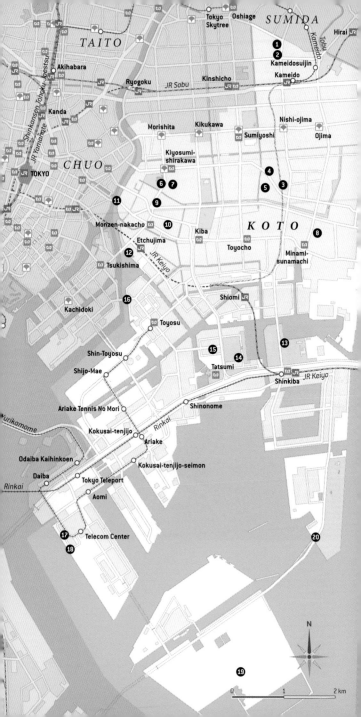

Koto

KATORI-JINJA SHRINE AT KAMEIDO

Shinto for sporting types

3-57-22 Kameido, Koto-ku (東京都江東区亀戸 3-57-22)
10-minute walk from Kameido station (亀戸), JR Sobu line
Open 9am–5pm daily

The Katori-Jinja Shinto shrine at Kameido (亀戸香取神社) is dedicated to victory and by extension has become the must-visit site for the capital's athletes. Allegedly founded in the 7th century, this is one of the shrines to Futsunushi, one of the sun goddess Amaterasu's generals mentioned in the *Nihon shoki*. Futsunushi is also a sword spirit in the Shinto pantheon. Since Fujiwara no Hidesato[1] bequeathed an arrow to the shrine after crushing Taira no Masakado's rebellion in the 10th century (see also p. 26) to give thanks to the *kami* (spirit or deity) for granting him victory, the shrine was the site of veneration of other great warriors, beginning with Chiba Shusaku.[2]

Competing at the Beijing Olympics in 2008, Izumi Hiroshi,[3] judo silver medal at Athens in 2004, was apparently carrying a *kachi-mamori* (勝守), a Shinto victory talisman (*omamori*), as did the women's volleyball team in the qualifying heats for the Athens Games.

Visit the shrine for the ambience rather than the architecture. On the small wooden plaques (*ema*) are written victory prayers or wishes for a particular game, or the whole season, an individual or team. In an eclectic atmosphere where all kinds of sporting types mingle freely, young baseball players rub shoulders with amateur boxers to make a quick offering at the weekend.

Note the imposing memorial shaped like a radish, with no sporting connotations but apparently offered to the shrine in the 19th century to give thanks for a bountiful harvest.

The pilgrims' road to the shrine, the oldest road in Koto, has a certain charm. The shopping street known as *Katori Daimon Shouun* (香取大門勝運商店街) was revamped without much fanfare in 2011 to give it a 1950s allure, with very successful results. There's something retro in the air, even if it's artificially revived.

NEARBY

Monument in the plum orchard ②

Utagawa orchard and Van Gogh

Behind Katori-Jinja shrine, along the banks of the Kita-Jikkengawa, a marker stone and noticeboard near No. 3-51 commemorate the site of Umeyashiki Park, where one of the most crooked plum trees in the city used to grow. The tree was first depicted by Utagawa Hiroshige[4] in the 19th century in *Umeyashiki* (梅屋敷 – Plum Orchard) from the series *One Hundred Views of Edo*, later recaptured by Van Gogh in his *Flowering Plum Orchard*. The park was destroyed in the great flood of 1910.

---

[1] *Nihon shoki (Chronicles of Japan) is a book of classical Japanese history, also known as* Nihon-gi.
[2] *藤原秀郷, ?–?, noble warrior at the 10th century court of Kyoto.*
[3] *千葉周作, 1793–1856, grand master of weapons and founder of the Hokushin Itto Ryu school.*
[4] *歌川広重, 1797–1858. Painter and grand master of* ukiyo-e *(art form popular in 17th–19th century Japan).*

REMAINS OF ONAGIGAWA CARGO TERMINAL

A huge terminal expunged in ten years

2-9 Kitasuna, Koto-ku (東京都江東区北砂 2-9)
20-minute walk from Nishi-Ojima station (大島), Toei subway Shinjuku line

Amysterious street name at a corner of Meiji-dori (小名木川駅前 – *Onagigawaeki-mae* – Onagigawa station), and a memorial with an actual train axle at Kitasuna 2-chome Park, are the only witnesses to the huge old station of Onagigawa, which has been totally wiped from the map over ten years.

A freight line cuts across the danchi of Kitasuna neighbourhood, barely concealing the gigantic Ario Kitasuna shopping centre.

Wherever an Ario emerges in the city, it's a good indicator of a former large industrial site that's been upgraded, as in the case of this former station, which opened in 1929.

It was closed in December 2000 and then dismantled. The shopping centre opened in 2010.

The site is a testament to the speed with which the city is changing. The centre, which is quite far from the subway, primarily serves the local neighbourhood, rather like a suburban monster "outlet".

Onagigawa Glover Kyo Bridge and Koto micro-dam
A cloverleaf bridge

North-west of the former freight station site, the crossing at right angles between the Yokojikkengawa and Onagigawa canals is topped by the magnificent Onagigawa Glover Kyo Bridge (小名木川グロバー橋 – Onagigawa Cloverleaf Bridge). This clover-shaped pedestrian bridge, built in 1994, is slightly domed to let the occasional boat pass below. Footfall is very light and the Sky Tree can easily be spotted to the north. Stop as you cross the bridge between the two canals, take a breather and soak up the atmosphere of the floating mists of Shitamachi. You'll see the south side of the Koto micro-dam, erected in 2015 on the Yokojikkengawa. This micro-dam, the first in Tokyo's twenty-three wards, produces a miniscule 1.1 kilowatts, only enough to power the night illumination of the bridge.

Sunamachi-Ginza
Spirit of the new Shitamachi

The east side of Meiji-dori is home to an alien, the shopping street of Sunamachi-Ginza (砂町銀座商店街), aka Sunagin, so different and thus so complementary to the modernity of the neighbouring Ario commercial centre.

Although far from the subways, and for all intents and purposes below sea level, the 600-metre street is popular and lively. The bombings wiped out the modest shopping street that was just emerging pre-war, and Sunagin was only commercialized in the 1960s in what was then an industrial zone.

Despite its youth, it has an old flavour, the scent of Shitamachi. You get the impression that the street has lived through the Edo period and it's only the façades that have been (very) loosely modernized. The rather narrow street is a fine example of the "new Shitamachi". Handwritten posters sometimes ask people not to publish the prices online and not to take photos for posting on social media.

CENTER OF THE TOKYO RAIDS AND WAR DAMAGE

A city under fire

1-5-4 Kitasuna, Koto-ku (東京都江東区北砂 1-5-4)
20-minute walk from Sumiyoshi (住吉) or Nishi-Ojima (大島) stations,
Toei subway Shinjuku line
Open 12 noon–4pm Wednesday to Sunday, closed Monday and Tuesday
Closed December 28 to January 4, always open 9 and 10 March

In the depths of Koto, a small brownstone building could pass for a house like any other were it not for the two statues at the entrance. In fact, this is home to the Center of the Tokyo Raids and War Damage (東京大空襲・戦災資料センター), a private museum that opened in its current form in 2007. It documents the incendiary bombing of Tokyo in 1945, especially the night of 9–10 March.

The museum, located far from the major attractions of the city centre, is not state-run and doesn't attract much media coverage, so it's not very busy. Don't be surprised to be the first visitor of the day, even at weekends. To be alone here only adds to the solemnity of the experience. Much of the display is in Japanese, but there's often no need for words.

The museum can pull at your heartstrings, and the statistics and maps showing the extent of the destruction may leave you speechless. The firestorm east of the Sumida, in particular, meant almost complete destruction. In one night, the entire district around the museum was razed to the ground: what you see now is a complete rebuild.

The museum also has a small collection of period documents, including propaganda leaflets dropped by the Americans, and various works of art reflecting the trauma of the event. It won't leave you unmoved.

The two statues at the entrance to the centre are particularly touching. *Sekai no kodomo no heiwazo* (世界の子どもの平和像 – Children's World Peace Statue) shows a child watering a sunflower with its face turned to the sun (symbolizing hope) in front of a large cracked egg, symbol of peace and fragility, which is about to hatch and give life. Alongside is the very moving *Senka no shita* (戦火の下 – In Time of War), showing a woman embracing her child.

NEARBY

Hayagriva of Koto ⑤
Monument to the horses killed in the bombing

A short walk south of the museum, at 1-3 Minamisuna on the east side of the block, a monument to the Buddhist deity Hayagriva ("Horse-headed") in a small stone enclosure bears the legend *Koto Batokanzeon* (江東馬頭観世音 – Stele of Hayagriva of Koto) engraved in red. The stele is dedicated to the 3,000 draught horses that died in the bombing. Every 10 March a discreet ceremony is held, recalling that the destruction of the city spared nothing and nobody.

SOCIAL HOUSING
AND COMMERCIAL PREMISES
ON KIYOSUMI AVENUE

Unique relic of the 1920s

3-3 Kiyosumi, Koto-ku (東京都江東区清澄 3-3)
5-minute walk from Kiyosumi-Shirakawa station (清澄白河), Tokyo metro
Hanzomon line, Toei subway Oedo line

Although any visitors to be seen around Kiyosumi-Shirakawa station are generally there for the popular Kiyosumi gardens, a row of around fifty houses (東京市営店舗向住宅) dating from 1928, along the west side of Kiyosumi avenue next to the gardens, is clearly worth a detour as a piece of early 20th century urban history.

These small two-storey concrete buildings (with some Art Deco details), part of the reconstruction of the city after the 1923 earthquake, are in very good condition, having miraculously survived the war and the ravages of time.

The buildings were originally very similar (shop on the ground floor, residential quarters upstairs), but were altered and repainted by successive occupants in the following decades – some people even added a floor or subtly altered the façade. Shops and smart cafés occupy some of the ground floors. The row still has a certain charm.

NEARBY
Kiyosumi gardens: founded by Mitsubishi ⑦

Although less well known than Koishikawa-Korakuen and without the striking contrasts of Hamarikyu, the attractive Kiyosumi gardens (清澄庭園) are laid out in the grounds of a domain acquired in 1878 and converted into gardens where employees could relax by the founder of the Mitsubishi group, Iwasaki Yataro.[1] An entrance fee is payable for the traditional east

side of the park, while the Western-style Kiyosumi Park on the west side (no pun intended) is open to all free of charge.

[1] 岩崎弥太郎, *1835–1885, born in the province of Tosa, became leader in 1870 of Tsukumo Shokai, a small trading company he renamed Mitsubishi Shokai, the forerunner of Mitsubishi group.*

LAND SUBSIDENCE OBSERVATION ⑧ CENTRE AT MINAMISUNAMACHI

The hollow below the city

3-14 Minamisuna, Koto-ku (東京都江東区南砂 3-14)
5-minute walk from Minamisunamachi station (南砂町), Tokyo metro
Tozai line
Observation centre closed to the public
Signs indicate subsidence

Subway passengers curious about their surroundings (it does happen…) will probably notice that the exits of Minamisunamachi station are slightly raised and the doors are much more massive than elsewhere. These doors are watertight to minimize the flood risk, as Minamisuna district is below the water level of Tokyo Bay.

Despite the station exit being approximately at sea level, you'll soon notice that the surroundings aren't flat and that some streets even slope downwards…!

Exit 2b leads to Minamisuna 3-chome Park, where a blue marker pole (水準標) shows the water levels when the area was inundated by the sea at low and high tides and by momentous storms and typhoons.

A little to the north of the park, along the street to the east near the baseball field, another marker pole stands next to a little hut. This is the land subsidence observation centre of Minamisunamachi (南砂町地盤沈下観測所), where two wells 130 metres and 70 metres deep were dug in 1954 and 1961 to measure the subsidence more precisely. The hollow below the city is most marked around here and the pole clearly indicates the levels of some very impressive tides.

A noticeboard explains the function of the wells, which are not accessible to the public.

One-fifth of Tokyo almost below sea level

To the east of the city, in Sumida, Koto, Edogawa and Katsushika wards, the flat land around the Arakawa is slowly sinking as human activity nibbles away and dries out the lower layers of the ground. Almost one-fifth of Tokyo is now below the water level in the bay. Some places in Koto have subsided 4.5 metres since 1918, when the first measurements were taken. This part of the city has turned into a vast basin which, just to complicate matters, is criss-crossed with watercourses at different heights – so the rate of subsidence is not uniform.

STAGING OF THE ENMA STATUE AT FUKAGAWA ENMADO

Sound-and-light show for donors

2-16-3 Fukagawa, Koto-ku (東京都江東区深川 2-16-3) in Fukagawa
Enmado temple (Hojoin)
10-minute walk from Monzen-Nakacho station (門前仲町), Tokyo metro
Tozai line, Toei subway Oedo line
Open 9am–5pm daily

About 500 metres north of Monzen-Nakacho, Hojoin temple houses a seated statue of *Enma*, which at 3.5 metres is one of the largest in Japan. Built in 1989 on the occasion of the restoration of the temple, the bright red wooden statue weighs 1.5 tonnes. It is in the building to the left of the entrance to the enclosure, the *enmado*. The temple complex is sometimes referred to as *Fukagawa Enmado* (深川ゑんま堂 – Enmado of Fukagawa).

Over and above its appearance and size, it is the staging of the statue that makes it so unusual: on each of the nineteen alms boxes set up in front of *Enma*, a different wish has been inscribed (academic success, marital happiness, etc.).

When someone throws in a donation, it sets off a brief sound-and-light show. *Enma*, with his severe countenance, then starts to preach in a deep voice at the often surprised follower, all under the projectors that will flash for some sermons.

Strengthen your legs in the footsteps of Soga Gogo

Inside Hojoin temple there's also a stone marked with footprints. According to legend these are the footprints of Soga Goro,[1] also known as Soga Tokimune.

Raised to the status of popular hero by the Kabuki play *Soga Monogatari* (曽我物語 – History of Soga), Goro and his brother tracked down his father's murderer. He finally killed him during the gigantic hunting party given in 1193 by Minamoto no Yoritomo[2] to celebrate his accession to the rank of shogun. The tradition is to stand on that stone to strengthen your legs.

[1] 曾我五郎, 1174–1193.
[2] 源頼朝, 1147–1199. Founder of the Kamakura shogunate.

FUKAGAWA FUDOU-DOU FAÇADE ⑩

Sanskrit inscription

1-17-13 Tomioka, Koto-ku (東京都江東区富岡 1-17-13)
Monzen-Nakacho station (門前中町), Tokyo metro Tozai line, Toei subway Oedo line
Open 8am–6pm except Ennichi days (縁日, every 1st, 15th and 28th of the month), when the temple closes at 8pm

I n Monzen-Nakacho, which is rarely visited by foreign tourists, stands the Fukagawa Fudou-dou Buddhist temple (深川不動堂), full name Naritasan Tokyo Betsuin Fukagawa Fudou-dou (成田山東京別院深川不動堂 – Tokyo Branch of Naritasan Temple). The temple, destroyed during the war, was rebuilt for the first time in the 1950s. A new main building has recently been erected in a particularly modern and highly original style. From a distance, it seems to be covered with a dark material that gradually reveals itself as you approach.

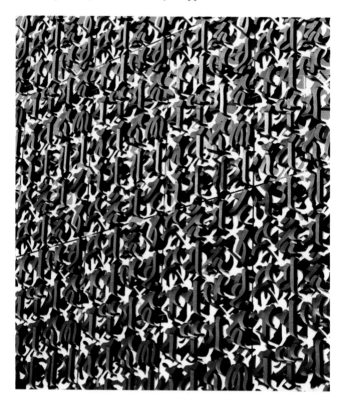

The façade of the temple, completed in 2011,[1] is completely covered with fine script in *Siddham* (Japanese 梵字 – *bonji*) to the most beautiful effect. Siddham is an alphabet that was used in northern India to transcribe Sanskrit around the 10th century, roughly the time of the widespread dissemination of Buddhism around Japan.

The partially gilded inscriptions repeat the mantra of the Buddhist fierce protective deity Acala-Vidyaraja, which reads (or is chanted) thus: *namah samanta-vajrânâm chanda mahârosana sphotaya hûm trat hâm mâm* (Homage to the all-pervading Vajras! O Violent One of great wrath! Destroy! *Hûm trat hâm mâm*).

The temple interior can be very animated, reflecting the tenacity of the Buddhist tradition.

The Fukagawa-Yawata festival, one of the "Big Three" Edo celebrations, is held every three years at the nearby Tomioka-Hachimangu shrine (富岡八幡宮), which commemorates the Tokyo bombing. The emperor visited the shrine in August 2012 and met some of the survivors, sixty-seven years after his father's visit shortly after the air raid on the city.

NEARBY

Eitaibashi ⑪

For a romantic evening near a replica of a German bridge

The Eitai Bridge (永代橋) over the Sumida, 10 minutes' walk from Monzen-Nakacho and Fukagawa Fudou-dou, was first erected in the late 17th century. Along with the Kiyosu Bridge it was rebuilt after the 1923 earthquake, a little south of its original site, crossing the Sumida just north of Tsukuda. The new bridge was modelled on the Ludendorff Bridge near Bonn, which collapsed in 1945, leaving only this replica, now classed as an Important Cultural Property.

In the evening, the bridge is illuminated with a lovely blue light. The night views of the bridge from either bank have their own charm – the west side, near the unmistakable twenty-five-storey IBM building at Hakozaki, is a little wider and greener. It's ideal for a leisurely stroll by day or night, either on your own or as a couple.

---

[1] *The extension works due for completion in autumn 2017 conceal some of the Siddham inscriptions.*

MEIJI MARU MUSEUM SHIP

19ᵗʰ century lighthouse tender moored in city centre

2-1-6 Echujima, Koto-ku (東京都江東区越中島 2-1-6)
Echujima station (越中島), JR Keiyo line
Accessible 24/7, at the time of writing the public not allowed on board

Crossing the Aioibashi from the artificial island of Tsukishima, you can't miss a magnificent three-masted vessel on the far bank: the *Meiji Maru* museum ship (明治丸), moored at the Echujima campus of Tokyo University of Marine Science and Technology (TUMSAT).

Built to service the newly built lighthouses of Meiji Japan, the *Meiji Maru* was commissioned from the Napier shipyard in Glasgow, Scotland, where it was launched in 1874 and sailed to Yokohama in 1875. The ship soon proved its worth to the Japanese Government – leaving Yokohama in 1876 at the same time as an English warship, it arrived two days earlier at Chichijima in the Ogasawara archipelago in the Pacific (Bonin Islands), bolstering Japan's territorial claim to the islands. A public holiday, Marine Day, was also inaugurated to commemorate the safe return of the Meiji Emperor to Yokohama on 20 July 1876, following his trip to the north of the country in the *Meiji Maru*.

The ship initially had only two masts – a third was added in 1898, when it was converted to a training ship. Although the interior of this superb museum, now classed as an Important Cultural Property, is closed to the public, ask at the university entrance to go into the campus to get a better look.

Several *yakatabune* (traditional boats offering tourist cruises) navigating the Sumida tie up opposite the *Meiji Maru* at nightfall. You can take this all in at a glance from the small Nakanoshima Park in the centre of Aioibashi. The surroundings are peaceful as Echujima, the station serving the campus, is the quietest on the JR East network, with a tiny fraction of the crowds that use Shinjuku station. Perfect for enjoying the incongruity of a 19th century ship in the city centre.

Unyo Maru: another sailing ship in the city

TUMSAT was established in 2004 following the merger of Tokyo University of Mercantile Marine (東京商船大学) with Tokyo University of Fisheries (東京水産大学). Each had its own Meiji-era ship moored on campus. The University of Mercantile Marine had the *Meiji Maru* and the University of Fisheries the *Unyo Maru* (雲鷹丸), a three-masted training ship dating from 1909. It is still moored at TUMSAT's Shinagawa campus at 4-5-7 Konan in Minato ward, where the University of Fisheries was based. You can see the ship's masts from the Monorail on the route between the city centre and Haneda Airport, although the hull is hidden by the urban expressway.

DAIGO FUKURYU MARU

On a former landfill site, a tuna boat irradiated in 1954

2-1-1 Yumenoshima, Koto-ku (東京都江東区夢の島 2-1-1) in Yumenoshima Park
10-minute walk from Shin-Kiba station (新木場), Tokyo metro Yurakucho line
Open 9.30am–4pm every day except Monday – if a public holiday falls on a Monday, the lobby is open, but closed the following day

Yumenoshima Park has a marina where a few yachts are moored, and a huge tropical greenhouse that will interest plant lovers. The park's most original attraction is undoubtedly the small tuna boat, *Daigo Fukuryu Maru* (東京都立第五福竜丸展示館).

This 141-tonne vessel belonging to Shizuoka prefecture, and launched in 1947, was typical of Japan's post-war fishing fleet. It was severely contaminated during the testing of a US atom bomb at Bikini Atoll[1] (Marshall Islands, North Pacific) in March 1954. Although the boat was in an area deemed safe at the time of the explosion, it was hit a few hours after the test by contaminated coral ash carried by the wind. It returned to port without incident after a few days, but a crew member died six months later as a result of irradiation.

The tuna boat, which is still in excellent condition, is now on public display in a small museum hall that doesn't take long to visit but is a fascinating reminder of the dangers of atomic weapons.

War of waste

With several sports facilities and a barbecue area, Yumenoshima Park is a peaceful, green oasis like several others along the bay. Hard to believe today that this site was once a vast open landfill for the whole capital, a hotbed of the famous "war of waste" between city wards in the 1970s.

In 1972, fed up with what was seen as Suginami's refusal to build a waste treatment centre, Koto decided to systematically block access to the site for Suginami dump trucks.

The malodorous picket line left a lasting impression.

For many Tokyoites, Yumenoshima is synonymous with "open-air dump", which might explain its relative tranquillity today.

[1] *Atoll of the Marshall Islands in the North Pacific.*

NEW SPORTS PARK AT TATSUMI NO MORI

Disc Golf and bowling in Tokyo

2-1-35 Tatsumi, Koto-ku (東京都江東区辰巳 2-1-35)
10-minute walk from Tatsumi station (辰巳), Tokyo metro Yurakucho line
Open 9am–5pm February to October, 9am–4pm November to January; closed
December 29 to January 3

At the southern end of Tatsumi no Mori koen (辰巳の森海浜公園), you can sometimes watch sporting types making odd gestures as they take part in rather surprising activities. This section of the park is reserved for eight "new sports".

It features a nine-hole *Mallet Golf* course, a sport somewhere between croquet and golf – a Japanese invention.

No iron or wood is needed for this new sport, just a mallet with a fairly large head that's very easy to handle.

In the same vein, *Disc Golf* involves throwing a disc into a special receptacle. There's also an eight-hole *Ground Golf* course, a version for older people using a larger ball.

Other versions include *Garden Golf*, developed right here, which uses billiard balls instead of the traditional ones; and *Putter Golf* (a variation on crazy golf), making it easy for young children to hit the ball.

Besides these courses, you'll find two *Free Tennis* courts (a sport that looks like giant table tennis) and *shuffleboard* courts (using cues to push

weighted discs around). There is even a petanque pitch, although far from any whiff of anise and the Mediterranean sun.

Apart from competition days, the place is rarely crowded and you can easily learn one of these new sports. Just book or simply say you want to use one of the courses, and hire the equipment you'll need. Some of the sports also offer introductory lessons in the mornings (sign up at the park information centre).

NEARBY

Tatsumi danchi ⑮

Relics of the 1960s along the bay

The gigantic Tatsumi *danchi* (辰巳団地) is just west of Tatsumi no Mori Park. Full name Tokyo Metropolitan Tatsumi 1-chome apartments (都営辰巳一丁目アパート), the Tatsumi *danchi* is key to understanding some of Tokyo's history.

His monster estate dating from the late 1960s, with around a hundred five-storey residential blocks (without lifts), clashes with the ultra-modern towers of Shinonome and Toyosu glittering in the background. The area completely missed out on the recent boom in megatowers along the shores of the bay and is stuck in its era. It was briefly in the limelight again during the 2011 earthquake as the soil liquefaction phenomenon was particularly obvious.

ABANDONED BRIDGE OF HARUMI ⑯

Relics of an abandoned freight line

Between 2 Harumi, Chuo-ku (東京都中央区晴海 2) and 2 Toyosu, Koto-ku (東京都江東区 2)
10 minutes from Toyosu station (豊洲), Tokyo metro Yurakucho or Yurikamome lines
Accessible 24/7 but bridge closed to the public

Crossing the Harumi canal near the family crowds at LaLaport shopping mall, the solitary Harumi Bridge (晴海橋梁) is a relic of a freight line from the days when the economy was booming.

It was built in 1957 to transport cement, raw materials and chemicals between Toyosu, Harumi and the Echujima cargo terminal. The increase in truck traffic made the line obsolete and it was finally abandoned in 1989, while Toyosu was being deindustrialized. The bridge is now closed to the public.

There are a few other relics of the line in the zone around the cargo terminal of Ecchujima, although the line itself has completely disappeared under the Toyosu concourse. Two pillars from a bridge dismantled in 2000 can be found on the Toyosu canal. East of the canal, at 1-Shiobara, the route of the line can clearly be seen south of the embankment, and farther south of 2-Shiobara the narrow overgrown strips show where it used to run.

Toyosu's industrial past

Toyosu (豊洲) has recently become one of the most noticeable spots in the city, but its past is more industrial, as borne out by the abandoned bridge. Like the neighbouring districts, Toyosu emerged from the waters of the bay in the first half of the 20th century. A number of factories were built there, including gas and power plants.

The closure of the power station in 1984, followed by the opening of Toyosu subway station and the end of gas production in 1988, accelerated the transformation of the district in the 90s. The factories gradually left the area, the workers' housing made way for offices, and then in 2000 and 2010 for monumental residential towers around Urban Dock LaLaport Toyosu, a shopping complex opened in 2006 on the site of an IHI corporation shipyard.

The breathtaking view of the Rainbow Bridge from the LaLaport restaurant terraces and a hint of sophistication in the air make it a popular venue, with a little-known past.

TOKYO CUSTOMS INFORMATION CENTRE ⑰

Contraband and "Custom-kun"

2-7-11 Aomi, Koto-ku (東京都江東区青海 2-7-11)
5-minute walk from Telecom Center station (流通センター),
Yurikamome line
Open 9am–5pm, closed weekends and public holidays
Admission free

On the second floor of Tokyo Customs main building, a novel information centre (東京税関・情報ひろば) features a series of small exhibitions on the history (since the arrival of Commodore Perry's "Black Ships" and the opening up of Japan), role and importance of customs for the country.

The centre has a selection of forgeries and various stuffed animals of protected species, sometimes beside some very imaginative examples of

smuggling methods. To top it all, after learning all about sniffer dogs, you can try out an X-ray machine simulator.

The centre does its best to try to strike a lighter note despite the serious theme – visitors can take selfies with the Customs mascot, Custom-kun, a cuddly yellow dog.

To enter the information centre, first register at the reception desk.

NEARBY

View of the Oi waterfront from Aomi Minami-Futo Park (18)

Waltz of the containers

A 5-minute walk from the Customs centre, just behind the touristic Oedo-Onsen-Monogatari, Aomi Minami-futo-koen is much quieter and often almost deserted. Fishing is allowed and keen anglers sometimes spend the whole day there. The park has a nice simple Japanese garden but above all offers one of the best views in town of the Oi container berths from the banks, to the delight of fans of port logistics and vast ships.

For those who want to enjoy the spectacular aspects of loading and unloading, come along in the morning when there's more movement of ships, and so more container activity.

Opposite, direct access to the Oi docks is out of bounds to the public and the giant cranes in the berths are only partially visible from the road. In addition, the truck traffic to and from the quays can soon become infernally noisy during rush hours. So much better enjoy it from a distance, in the park.

The bay on the Oi side is an ode to cargo ships: the seven berths are served by fourteen red and white cranes, covering 2,354 metres of the shoreline. These docks, opened in 1975 and renovated in 2004, are the largest of the three cargo docks in Tokyo Port.

The "historical" docks, opened in 1967, are at Shinagawa, just north of Oi. With only three berths, these are the smallest docks in the port. The third site is at Aomi, next to the park. Every year, around 3,000 cargo ships and 1.8 million TEU containers transit through Oi.

On the other side of the water at Oifuto, Minatogaoka-Futo-koen, opened in 1977, is a public park run by Tokyo Port. In the centre of the park is a 20-metre artificial hill – high enough for a good view of the area, including part of the docks.

CHUO-BOHATEI LANDFILL

The city covers its waste

5 minutes from Kankokyoku-Chuo-Godochoshamae bus stop (環境局中防合同庁舎前); Toei subway line 波1 from Telecom Center station (テレコムセンター), Yurikamome line
Accessible 24/7, last bus from Telecom Center 9pm
Booking required (http://www.tokyokankyo.jp/kengaku/umetate.html or 03-3570-2230) to visit a processing plant
Tours available 9am–4.30pm Monday to Friday, plus Saturdays in January, February, March, July and August

Among recent major projects in the bay, the Chuo-Bohatei (中央防波堤 – Central Breakwater) landfill is a good example of the city's genesis: 300 hectares of Tokyo reclaimed from the water. Just after the Chuo-Ohashi Bridge, there's a small space alongside the road (accessible to anyone with the courage to walk along here) below the landing and takeoff trajectories of Haneda Airport's runway B.

The maritime landfill zone itself is normally inaccessible to the public, but the Tokyo Metropolitan Environmental Corporation (東京都環境公社) organizes tours to a processing plant on the north side of the landfill. The visit gives you an idea of what happens to waste and the role it plays in the city's expansion.

NEARBY

Pedestrian access to the Gate Bridge ⑳

The majestic Gate Bridge (ゲートブリッジ), opened in February 2012 to connect Chuo-Bohatei and Wakasu, is partially accessible to pedestrians via the southern tip of Wakasu.

Completed in the mid-1970s, this is incidentally one of the city's few administrative districts with no official residents.

A bus runs through the area, linking the south exit of Shin-Kiba station to the campsite in Wakasu Park, one of the few within Tokyo Metropolis. The campsite is lively at the weekends and during summer barbecues. The bus runs alongside an authentic eighteen-hole golf course, Golf Links, under protective nets in case of stray balls.

The campsite and golf course are in the shadow of the impressive bridge structure.

An elevator takes you up to the deck, where you can enjoy an unobstructed view of the east of the city. Note that only the eastern section is open to pedestrians, so you can't cross over to the Chuo-Bohatei landfill if you're on foot.

Anime, アニメ, cartoons.

Apato (from "apartment"), アパート, a generally low (two- or three-storey) collective residence with a wooden or light steel structure, particularly popular during the Showa period. The generally limited space in this type of housing and the thinness of the walls led to these emblematic Japanese collective residences of the 1960s and 70s being nicknamed "rabbit cages".

Bodaiji, 菩提寺, Buddhist temple used for family funeral ceremonies.

Bunrei, 分霊, division of a *kami* (Shinto deity) to produce two copies of the original, in order to transfer one copy to another shrine site.

Combini (from "convenience store"), コンビニ, local shop, usually a chain franchise.

Cosplay, コスプレ, disguise as a manga or game character.

Dagashi, 駄菓子, cheap candy treats, mainly sold to children.

Daikokuten, 大黒天, Buddhist protective deity, from the Sanskrit name *Mahakala*, derived from the Hindu god *Shiva*. One of the seven gods of happiness.

Daimyo, 大名, feudal lord.

Danchi, 団地. The *danchis* are a functional category of housing in urbanization plans. They are mainly used as public or semi-public residential complexes for less affluent social strata. Normally very easy to spot, they are enormous alignments of concrete blocks of the same height, where utility is more important than appearance. The big *danchis* were developed after World War II and during the subsequent economic boom.

Datsue-ba, 奪衣婆, demonic entity stripping the spirits of the dead as they cross the Sanzugawa (三途川), the river at the gateway to the underworld.

Doya-gai, ドヤ街, "doya neighbourhood", a district offering basic accommodation for the night at very low prices. The word doya is slang, an inversion of *yado* (宿), housing.

Ebisu, 恵比寿, protective deity, god of fishing, one of the seven gods of good fortune, the only Japanese divinity without a Hindu origin.

Ema, 絵馬, small wooden plaque in Shinto sanctuaries where you can write a prayer or wish.

Enma, 閻魔, Buddhist and Hindu deity, *Yama*, judges the dead at the entrance to the underworld.

Gachagacha, ガチャガチャ, also called *Gachapon* (ガチャポン), coin-operated distributor of toys in a plastic capsule, echoing the noise when you turn the handle after inserting a coin.

Genkai-shuraku, 限界集落 ("beyond the pale"), rural or mountain village far from the country's main trade routes, where the ageing population threatens the very existence of the village.

Geta, 下駄, traditional footwear.

Goemon-buro, 五右衛門風呂, cast-iron bathtub heated directly by a fire, with a wooden plate to avoid direct contact with the hot surface.

Hatamoto, 旗本, samurai in direct service of the shogunate during the Edo period.

Hatsumode, 初詣, first prayers of the Japanese New Year.

Hokora, 祠, Shinto shrine, a secondary sanctuary.

Honetsugi, 骨接ぎ, traditional chiropractor or bone setter.

Hotei, 布袋, laughing Buddha, divinity of tolerance and generosity.

Hondo, 本堂, main hall of a temple, housing the subject of veneration.

Irori, 囲炉裏, Japanese traditional fireplace.

Izakaya, 居酒屋, "gastropub", something between a bar and a restaurant, alcohol always available.

Jizo, 地蔵, one of the most revered Buddhist bodhisattvas in Japan, *Kshitigarbha* is his Sanskrit name. Often represented in the form of a standing monk, he is identified in popular belief as a saviour of wandering souls and spirits, sometimes the protector of children.

JMA, *Kishocho*, 気象庁, Japan Meteorological Agency.

JSDF, Jieitai, 自衛隊, Japan Self-Defense Forces.

Kabayaki, 蒲焼き, grilled eel.

Kagai or **hanamachi** (花街), red-light district where the geisha establishments are located.

Kami, 神, Shinto spirit or deity.

Kanzashi, 簪, hair decorations.

Koban, 交番, neighbourhood police station.

Kojiki, (古事記, Records of Ancient Matters) and **Nihonshoki** (日本書紀, Chronicles of Japan). Both date from the 8th century and are considered the earliest official histories of Japan. Among other details, they present myths and legends about the foundation of the country and describe the essence of the Shinto pantheon.

Konnyaku, こんにゃく, paste made from konjac flour.

korokke (from Dutch *Krokket*), コロッケ, fried croquettes, usually based on mashed potatoes, a Japanese speciality inspired by Western cuisine that appeared at the end of the 19th century.

Manekineko, 招き猫, cat statuette inviting good fortune.

Mansion, マンション, collective housing.

Miko, 巫女, woman in the service of a shrine.

MLIT, *Kokudo Kotsusho* 国土交通, Ministry of Land, Infrastructure, Transport and Tourism.

Moba-Moga, モボ・モガ, abbreviation of "Modern Boy, Modern Girl", culture and fashion of Westernized youth starting in the 1920s and 30s.

Mon, 紋, heraldic sign.

Monjayaki, もんじゃ焼き, speciality made from wheat flour.

Monozukuri, ものづくり, "manufacture of things", a term often used to highlight Japanese precision engineering and industrial production.

Nihonshoki, see *Kojiki*.

Omamori, 御守, protective talisman.

Oyakodon, 親子丼, bowl of rice covered with an egg mixture.

Pachinko, パチンコ, arcade ball game resembling pinball.

Rakans, 羅漢, disciples of Buddha on the path of Enlightenment (*arhat*), often represented with a comic expression.

Rangakusha, 蘭学者, "Hollandologist", Japanese intellectuals of the Edo period specializing in the study of Western texts obtained, *inter alia*, through trade with Dutch navigators during the country's isolationist period.

Romaji, ローマ字, Roman alphabet.

Ronin, 牢人 or 浪人, in the Edo period, warrior without a master following the loss (or abandonment) of his feudal lord.

Ryotei, 料亭, upmarket establishment, sometimes with geisha in attendance.

Sando, 参道, pilgrimage route, path from *torii* to shrine.

Sento, 銭湯, public baths.

Shomen-Kongo, 青面金剛, six-armed blue deity, Yaksha spirit derived from Chinese Taoism and the heart of the popular *Koshin* cult (庚申). Shomen-Kongo is a god-demon protecting against disease.

Shugoshin, 守護神, guardian, protective deity.

Shukuba, 宿場, rest stop on the Edo routes (see p. 155).

Sobas, 蕎麦, buckwheat noodles.

Suikinkutsu, 水琴窟, traditional garden ornament, acting as a musical instrument based on the sound of drops of water falling into a hidden underground chamber.

Tokusatsu, 特撮, TV series or film with many special effects (ranging from *Bioman* to *X-Or* and *Godzilla*), *Ultraman* being one of the earliest of the genre.

Torii, 鳥居, gateway to a Shinto shrine.

Wadokei, 和時計, mechanical clock giving traditional time (see p. 21). The variable length of hours in the Edo period, according to the seasons, gave rise to some particularly complex devices.

Yakatabune, 屋形船, traditional pleasure boat used for dining cruises.

Zaibatsu, 財閥, industrial and financial conglomerate.

PHOTOGRAPHY CREDITS
All rights reserved. Photos by Pierre MUSTIÈRE, with the exception of:

David MICHAUD :
Criminology section of Meiji University Museum (p. 16), Takarakuji Dreamkan (p. 30), Okuno building (p. 32), Toyokawa-Inari temple (p. 42), Kagata shrine (p. 60), Tamagawa-Daishi exterior (p. 121)

Nesnad, Kyu-Furukawa gardens (p. 148)

Wiii, Tokyo Mosque (p. 186)

Construction of Komatsugawa lock (New Year card, c. 1930, p. 216)

Great Buddha of Ueno, Taisho era, 1912–1926 (p. 247)

Views of Asakusa and Azumabashi after March 1945 bombardment. Thanks to the Center of the Tokyo Raids and War Damage for these photographs (p. 253 and p. 255)

ILLUSTRATIONS
Meeting between William Adams and Tokugawa Ieyasu in 1600, Pieter VAN DER AA, 1707 (p. 24)
Poster for Tokyo's 1940 Expo (p. 37)
徳川幕府刑事図譜 (illustrated book of penalties from the Tokugawa shogunate, 1893) (p. 67 and p. 271)
木曾街道板橋之驛 (Itabashi stop on the Kiso-kaido route), KEISAI Eisen (渓斎英泉), c. 1836 (p. 155)
名所江戸百景 四ツ木通用水引ふね (One Hundred Famous Views of Edo: Towboats Along the Yotsugi-dori Canal),
UTAGAWA Hiroshige (歌川広重), 1857 (p. 202 and cover),
Extension of Tokyo into the bay, Pierre MUSTIÈRE, various sources, 2017 (p. 213)
幻燈写心競 隅田川 (Daydreams by Magic Lantern: Sumidagawa), TOYOHARA Chikanobu (豊原周延), 1890 (p.258)
Mantra Mahāpratyangirā, 10th century BC (p. 285)

ACKNOWLEDGEMENTS
KERA Hiyoko, Machiko and Yuichiro; Nadine MUSTIÈRE; Nicolas PLARD; Carole NAGANUMA; KANNO Naoko; SANO Kana; Samir BENNAFLA; Stéphanie AYUSAWA; Marine DURAND; Mamoun DRISSI KACEMI; Miku, Annie, Asuka and Momo in Baltimore; for corrections, clarifications and/or authorizations: KAWAKAMI Yusuke (Minato City Local History Museum, p. 47); HORI Kenshin (Gohyaku Rakan-ji, p. 58); YASUDA Kiyotaka (Food and Agriculture Museum, p. 104); TAKADA Hiroshi (Koyama-Shuzo brewery, p. 141); ISHII Naoe (Arakawa Museum of Aqua, p. 144); KITAGAWA Shoichiro (Kyu-Furukawa gardens, p. 148); ISHIDA Tsuyoshi (Tsumami-Kanzashi Mini Museum, p. 162); MIYAZAWA Satoshi (Shinjuku Historical Museum, p. 168); AMITANI Norimasa (Kokugakuin University, p. 180); KASUGA Ryo (Shogan-ji, p. 210); MURAKI Megumi (Tokyo Waterworks Historical Museum, p. 232); special thanks to FUTABA ryotei and Kingyo for introducing me (p. 258); KUMAGAI Katsuhiro (The Seiko Museum, p. 262); ICHIDA Mari (Daigo Fukuryu Maru museum hall, p. 288); SHIBATA Junko (Tokyo Customs Information Centre, p. 294); LEE Kazuo (Tokyo Metropolitan Environmental Corporation, p. 296); even though the places concerned have not been included in this edition for reasons of space, we are grateful for the assistance of FUJITA Teru (Suginami Animation Museum), SAWA Yoshihiro, MISAKA Mihoko (Training Centre at Tokyo-Rinkai Disaster Prevention Park) and WADA Tadashi (Tokyo Subway Museum).

Maps: : **Cyrille Suss** - Layout Design: **Coralie Cintrat** - Layout: **Iperbole**
English translation: **Caroline Lawrence** - Editing and proofreading: **Jana Gough and Eleni Salemi**

© JONGLEZ 2017
Registration of copyright: June 2017 – Edition: 01
ISBN : 978-2-36195-115-3
Printed in Bulgaria by Multiprint